MOTHER'S

An Essay Collection

by Park Young-ja

IMAGE LITERATUR

Wilshire Blvd. Suite #300
Los Angeles, CA 90010 U.S.A
Tel: 213-761-0880

ISBN: 978-0-9745105-2-1

First Edition 2007
Printed in Seoul, Korea

Dedicated to my mother,
may she rest in peace···

Author's Notes

I started writing late in my life. For this reason, I have been self-conscious about jumping into the literary world. Notwithstanding my reckless attempt, it has taken me ten years to work up enough courage to publish my first essay collection, and now I am about to send another book out into the world—in English, no less—as I turn seventy years old.

I am a nervous wreck, not knowing how my collection of memories will fare outside my country, especially this day and age when the world is changing at such a hurried pace. I try to take comfort in thinking that our high-tech world still needs the voice of a wildflower like me, no matter how fragile and meager.

I have always identified myself with a wildflower among trees. I see hidden strength of life in the wildflower and I take courage from it. I only wish that this book reflects that courage, and that it helps readers understand some aspects of Korean sensibilities.

I want to thank all those who have made it possible for me to publish this edition, including John Cha for his translation work.

May, 2007
Park Young-ja
e-mail : jenny40112@hotmail.com

Table of Contents

The Sea

I had long dreamed about living in a house of my own with an ocean view, and now I do. In my hometown, Jeju Island. I am glad that I no longer have to impose on my relatives, which I used to do whenever family matters called for my presence on the island.

My grown children are concerned that I am here alone. They call me and ask, "Aren't you lonely?" But I never feel lonesome. Actually, I rather enjoy my solitude, free to read and write as I like, a peace of mind, long overdue.

I like the fact that the ocean is right outside my door. I throw on a sweater and step out in my tennis shoes and I am on the beach. The warm sun on my shoulders makes me think that winter is gone, but the wind penetrating through my clothes tells me that

Jeju Island, southern coast

spring hasn't arrived quite yet. The light sea breeze makes waves over the quiet garlic fields, and the garlic scent follows my footsteps along the dirt path. The dirt pathway gives way to an asphalt pavement that leads me to a posh hotel, and the contrast makes me feel as though I have walked through two distinct worlds, one civilized and the other, untamed.

Cars stream by, spewing exhaust fumes like they do in Seoul, yet the smell doesn't strike me as harsh. Palm trees line the median strip like soldiers in formation and in between the trees a banner hangs flapping with bold letters, "APEC 2005 in Jeju, Free International Trade Zone!"

I wonder what our ancestors would think about the burgeoning international city, those poor souls who had gone to sea for their livelihood only to perish in angry storms? An old man who had been following me from way behind passes ahead of me. On his back, he is hauling a plastic fertilizer bag filled with old vegetables, eggshells, and old fruits. He doesn't fit in with the manicured city built to attract tourists, and I catch up to him and ask where he is going.

He appears annoyed by my question as he replies in his crude Jeju dialect, "To fertilize my field." And he moves on proudly. I don't know who he is, but he appears to be the proud caretaker of a land that had been handed down for generations.

I follow down the road about ten meters towards the sign Woman Diver's House to see the breakwater and the open sea beyond. The sea is dead calm, and a dark cloud glides over the horizon in the distance with fishing boats floating on it. As a poet once said, I can almost grab and pull the horizon towards me. And I recall a verse from Paul Lacroute's poem, "I can open my mind only to you."

The endless sea and its vast body of water are a reminder for my meager existence and I am ashamed of my egotistical ways in the past. The sea is a quiet teacher; its gentle waves roll in, showing us how to embrace all things, living or dead. And the tall waves gather momentum as they reach the shore, then crash, spraying water drops high in the sky. The water drops land on the beach, cast white foam on the sand, and recede, leaving behind only silent stillness until the next one comes.

I watch the waves roll in over and over and I think that the waves are admonishing my egotistical existence characterized by my inner struggles – my frustrations, anger, anxiety, agony, regrets, and guilt. The waves seem to say that I create these afflictions for myself, spoiled by all the modern conveniences. I recall a priest say that the dying commonly regret at the final moment of their lives: "I should have been more kind... more forgiving... more patient."

As I stand mesmerized by the sea, I wonder what was going through Hendrik Harmel's mind, the wayward Dutch sailor who had survived the crash in the storm and drifted to Jeju Island on August 16, 1653. What was he thinking about as he looked out to the same ocean before me? Was he thinking about his failed attempt at finding gold in Asia? Did he long for his hometown? Is that why he escaped in the middle of a night after living here for decades? Most likely, he wanted to live out his life without regrets and he felt compelled to leave Jeju. He hadn't heard what I'm hearing now: the silent words of the sea and the universal truth in those sounds. It tells me to devote myself to studying before I get too much older.

I wonder why I hear those words, why I should devote myself to doing anything at my age. Is it because of the sense of incompleteness I feel? Or, do I feel cheated by the harsh life I had gone through and that I need to compensate for those years? Confucius told us to stop learning at the age of sixty, and I could easily take this advice and live a life of leisure without worrying about anything else.

Yet I feel compelled to write and sit in front of the computer every night, hoping to write the words thicker than the color of the sea. With my fingers on the keyboard, however, I see only the flickering empty screen, not the flowing words. And I feel that my expectations and desire far exceed my capability. No one cares if I write or not, and it would be simple to stop it any time. What a fool I am, however. I feel I must continue writing; it is easier for me to deal with the struggles of writing than deciding not to write at all. So I press on to define the life's lessons the sea gives me, the roar of the storm or the sound of silence that I have only begun to realize and feel through my writing.

I didn't pay much attention to the actual sounds of the sea when I was growing up. I recall holding my mother's warm hand as we stood looking out to the sea endlessly. I miss those carefree days, when I didn't hear the painful sounds that I'm hearing now, as I stand here trying to convince myself that the word "love" is not a stationary noun but a moving verb. Like the ebb and flow of waves, you see and feel it after it has come and gone.

Jeju Women

Going to Jeju Island is a major event for some people. I, on the other hand, make the trip on a regular basis whenever there is a gathering with my husband's family there. Each time I get off the airplane, I am struck by the salty smell of the ocean breeze. The familiar rows of palms sway a welcome bow, and I gaze out to the endless sea and rest my eyes on the myriad shades of turquoise and emerald. Cows graze on idyllic meadows in between lush tangerine orchards. I marvel at the pristine Jeju scenery, a picture of perfect harmony between man and nature.

I feel fortunate every time I put my feet down in my husband's hometown. It has been my hometown for quite some time now, and I have developed a longing for it. Longing for hometown is like a longing for mother's embrace, they say, although no hometown is going to equal my mother.

I first learned about Jeju Island in grade school. My teacher told me that a god of trinity (Yang, Goh, and Bu) founded Jeju in the ancient times, and that there were many expressions involving number 3. I also heard that homes in Jeju didn't have any chimneys so as not to give away their position to invaders from Mongolia. The absence of a chimney saturated the kitchen with smoke, depositing black soot on all the utensils and cookware, which Jeju women dutifully cleaned and scrubbed until they shined. I always thought Jeju was a backward place in terms of culture. I never dreamed that I would marry a man from Jeju.

Someone described Halla Mountain of Jeju as feminine while characterizing Sorak Mountain as male. Mountainous features influence the personality of the people, evidenced by the gentle features of the Halla and the generous nature of the people of Jeju. More than anything, I can feel the nature of the Jeju people from the three long poles standing by the stone post at the entrance to their homes. The resident lowers down one pole when he or she goes away for a little while; two poles to indicate absence of half-day. Three lowered poles mean that the house is empty. I envy the way they tell their neighbors about their homes, their open way of life.

Today, I am going to my nephew's wedding. I choose to drive on an open road rather than through a downtown area riddled with tall buildings. I try to enjoy the scenery whenever I get a chance, and extra time for the detour is worth the effort. Near my nephew's house, I meander through an alley fenced by black lava rocks on both sides. I arrive at my nephew's house to the smell of food cooking. The women in the kitchen are filling plates and bowls with food and laughing. The men in the courtyard greet me in thick Jeju dialect, "How you been," and "Why you come so late?" Their voices are full of affection. The entire neighborhood is there to celebrate. My sister-in-law, the groom's mother, moves about frantically, muttering her worries about whether ten pigs and five sacks of rice are enough food for everyone.

I have always considered myself capable enough to stay up with anyone in preparing for events like this, but I can't match these Jeju women. Their team of twenty to thirty women is managing the gathering of several hundred people like it was nothing. The women move about happily, with no sign of pressure in anyone. They are sturdy as rocks, Jeju's foundation. When I first got married, I was ashamed to tell my friends that Jeju was my new hometown. But now, I wait for someone to ask me where my hometown is.

My sister-in-law comes over and grabs my hand and says, "Welcome, welcome." Her hand is firm and a bit rough, and I feel her affection rushing into my veins. Too, I can feel in her hand the energy that has transformed Jeju from a ramshackle village to a thriving community with visitors from all over the world.

I offer her to help her, and she shakes her head, no, the women from the neighborhood have everything under control.

The celebration goes on in earnest. People dive into the food, pour drinks for each other, sing songs, make speeches, and laugh endlessly.

Before we know it, the moon comes up over the trees, signaling the end to the daylong celebration. Men stagger away satisfied. Women stay and clean up and put away the leftover food as they sing.

Everyone is gone and my sister-in-law and I retire to her room. She feels good about the way the day went, and she starts tracing her old daysthe war days and the way brothers took arms against each other on account of the differences in ideology and other such things. She recounts who had died and who is still missing, an old neighbor lady who is still waiting for her son's return. Hungry days, sad days. "My poor children. They wanted to eat white rice badly. There was a *jesa*. Someone made white rice, and my kids saw it and waited and waited until the *jesa* was over. They fell asleep, missed their chance. They cried and cried."

She sighs in the dark and continues, "One time we stayed up all night delivering a calf. When we found out that it was a female, we thought we had received a gift from heaven." We keep on talking into the wee hours of the night.

I tell her about my first encounter with the ancient Jeju toilette. "It had no walls, and I was so embarrassed to squat in the open."

She laughs.

I continue, "Those terrible toilettes are long gone and disappeared, and I don't know why but I miss it."

She laughs aloud again. I sense in her laughter that my hardships were nothing compared to hers. She had raised three kids by tilling the volcanic soil with her hands literally. Tenant farming in Jeju was indeed a hard way to go, and I could never match her in perseverance and endurance.

I take her wrinkled hand and offer to trim her fingernails. The old woman warrior says, "Don't worry about my nails. All I have to do is to work a little. That's how I trim my nails."

I look at her and tell her that she should come and live with me instead of living alone. She replies, "The tradition in Jeju is—I live on my own, from my kids or anyone else, until I reach my time to part this world, when my oldest son comes and takes me to his house for my funeral."

She smiles, and I see no trace of regret in her eyes. I see a nameless plant that grows green in the wild and comes back year after year despite the desolate conditions it had faced. I am in awe of the Jeju woman.

Jeju women divers

Winter Kimchi

The familiar chill is in the air, cleansed by the late autumn drizzle, a signal for me to make winter kimchi. There is no time to take in fall's splendor leisurely. Winter kimchi has been on my mind since immediately after chuseok harvest celebration, the way it has been for me every year ever since I started my own family. And this year marks the forty-third.

Making winter kimchi used to be a big event for housewives, a tradition as significant as the chuseok celebration. People buy packaged kimchi at stores now, and making winter kimchi is no longer a tradition; it is merely an option. I still make my own winter kimchi, not because of the tradition or habit. Winter kimchi means more than fermented cabbage to me; it is a way for me to trace my past and preserve the memories.

Memories that begin with bright red peppers and sweet tangy garlic stalks...

I go to the open marketplace, a fairground humming with hawking merchants, shoppers in search of the best deals. The sweet aroma emanating from mounds of dried red pepper, garlic stalks, and fresh cabbage generate frenzied energy all around the marketplace, and no one notices the pristine autumn sky.

I thread myself through the crowd in front of the red pepper stand and pick out the brightest one. I smell it first, squeeze it, then smell it again. It is too dry. I drop it back in the pile and pick out another. The smell stings my nose, makes my mouth water. I squeeze it between my thumb and pointer finger. It doesn't crumble, but it's still too dry. I go to the next stand, and the next. After checking all the red pepper stands, I move on to garlic stands.

I only have enough money for red pepper and garlic at this time. The cabbage, the most expensive ingredient, will have to wait until my husband's payday. When we were just the two of us, I bought two hundred pieces of cabbage, which were enough to last through the year. Steamed rice and kimchi were the main staples for us, then and many years following. Our family has grown to five, and I shop for about five hundred pieces of cabbage. On my husband's payday, I go back to the marketplace and check the stacks of cabbage in earnest. The cabbage stacks appear every morning and they are sold and gone by afternoon. After one day's time, I know which merchant has the best cabbage for the least amount of money. I wait for the fresh stacks of cabbage the following morning and I make the deal. That afternoon, they deliver the load of cabbage to my home. I am ready now to prepare a year's worth of kimchi. I look at the mound of cabbage in the middle of the courtyard and I feel the adrenaline flowing inside me. My family won't go hungry for a year with the kimchi I'm about to make. We will have enough kimchi to eat with rice three meals a day.

Often, the first snowfall comes about the time I finish making kimchi and fill the jars buried in the yard. I welcome the snow and I am smug knowing that we're ready for the winter. The earthen jars will keep the temperature even for our kimchi. I am reminded of a legend from the ancient times when our ancestors used to sustain life with nothing but grass roots and tree barks. They chopped up pine leaves, mixed it with radish and cabbage, and fermented the mixed green in brine. They called it song-jeo (pine kimchi) and ate it once a day to alleviate hunger pain.

Kimchi's role has changed over the centuries. No longer a hunger pain reliever, kimchi is a research subject for nutritionists around the world. Many internationally renowned chefs tout the unique delicacy. Among the hundreds of types of kimchi, bossam kimchi is the crown jewel with luscious ingredients like gingko nuts, pine nuts, walnuts, and eight different fruits all together. And there are kimchis made of vegetables other than cabbage: radish leaf kimchi, white radish kimchi in water, red radish kimchi, Korean lettuce kimchi, cucumber kimchi, eggplant kimchi, pumpkin kimchi, spinach kimchi, and sesame leaf kimchi.

The nutritionists analyze and measure the ingredients and try to replicate various types of kimchi, only to find out that scientific methods do not produce consistent taste, mystifying many foreign chefs. So they are left with the conclusion that there's more to kimchi taste than just recipes and technique. There is an intangible ingredient, an element of the heart, an immeasurable warmth that flows from the heart to the fingertips. No weighing scale is adequate for measuring experienced eyes, hands, and taste.

Likewise, in matters of life, preciseness is a quality to be admired. Yet precision often contradicts the warmth that we need and crave.

Sharing a meal is one of those warm moments. Food tastes better when everyone hovers together over a small table. Place a stalk of ripened winter kimchi in the middle of the table and watch the children's tiny fingers grab and tear off a long string of cabbage leaf, toss their heads back, and thread the string into their mouths, followed by a spoonful of steaming hot rice. They yelp HOT, HA, and giggle as they chew.

That was a lifetime ago.

A few months ago, my son, daughter, their spouses, and children came over and saw me marinating cabbages in salt water. My son nagged and nagged at me like a noisy cicada in the heat of summerall you have to do is just push the buttons on the telephone, and they'll deliver all the kimchi you want. Why do you insist on going against the tide of time?

So I relented and ordered some kimchi over the telephone. I didn't want my grandchildren to remember me as a stubborn old woman.

The kimchi came shortly like my son had said. In a plastic bag like a bag of chips.

I stared at the slick package sitting on the table for a long time, appalled. That's not it, that's not it, I repeated to myself. I am receptive to progress in general, but my world has turned upside down, and I felt like I had lost my place in life. That was my first and the last time I ordered kimchi over the telephone.

Call me stubborn, call me old fashioned, but I am not about to cast aside all those years of memories as a wife and mother in the name of progress. Those memories are mine, mine only, and I have a right to hang on to them.

I mix ground red pepper, chunks of ginger and garlic in anchovy sauce.

My daughter-in-law chops green onions, mustard green, miniature green onions, and parsley at finger-lengths. My daughter makes thin slices of radish.

I take a leaf of cabbage and wrap it with a fresh oyster dressed in anchovy sauce and hold it up for my daughter-in-law to taste. She takes it in her mouth and nods her approval. It is mild, just the right taste for her family.

Now we are ready to stuff the sauce mix inside the cabbage. I check the basin filled with cabbage stalks cut in halves. The twenty or so cabbages (not five hundred like the old days) have been marinating in salt-water overnight and they look tender and pale, ready for rinsing.

My daughter fills a new basin with fresh water. We take out the cabbage halves soaking in salt-water and put them in the fresh water and rinse them. My daughter-in-law drains salt-water from the old basin and refills it with fresh water. We transfer the cabbages into the fresh water and rinse it again.

I tear off a piece of the rinsed cabbage and taste it. It is crunchy and a bit salty. One more rinse, and we squeeze the cabbages dry and shake off excess water from each one as we pile them in a mound.

I take a cabbage, put it down on the board on its back with its inside face up showing many layers of stems, pale white with streaks of light yellow, and I fill the space in between its layers with dripping red stuffing. The red comes from the ground cayenne pepper, introduced to Korea in the sixteenth century, rather recent in terms of the history of kimchi. The red pepper and its magical juice keep the kimchi crunchy and fresh for months.

After the first batch, we work on the second batch, a bit saltier than the first, for my daughter's family. I add more anchovies and juice to the sauce, and we take turns tasting it. My daughter taste it, smiles, and says yes and we continue stuffing cabbages with the new sauce. By this time, we're comfortable with the routine and we chat away as we move our hands between the cabbage leaves and the sauce.

I tell them how people used to measure a woman's worth by the taste of the kimchi she produced. The young women ask me about my kimchi, and I reply that my kimchi was regarded excellent and that I was in a class by myself. I tell them how people used to praise me and call me a devoted homemaker.

They laugh heartily. In their laughter I sense puzzlement: what's kimchi got to do with womanhood?

I don't know how to explain the connection to them, nor the tremendous sense of accomplishment I had felt each time after making winter kimchi. I tell them, you're lucky you don't have to make winter kimchi every year.

The young women nod in agreement, and the conversation turns to another subject. They talk about their children, my favorite topic. I can never hear enough about my grandchildren, and before we know it, we are done making kimchi.

My daughter packs her kimchi in jars, and my daughter-in-law does the same. They will take their kimchi home and store it in the kimchi refrigerator for the fermenting process. We put the rest in jars for storing in my refrigerator.

We clean and put away all the paraphernalia that go with making kimchi, and I say to them, job well done. They breathe a sigh of relief and smile.

I watch the young women walking towards their cars holding a bag with kimchi in it in one hand and their children's hand in the other. It is a picture of happiness, and my heart glows warm. All we need is the first snow of the season to make it a perfect day.

Mosquito

The summer heat can be unbearable, but worse, its humidity brings out the torturous mosquitoes. Flies are annoying insects as well, but I think the mosquitoes are more deplorable because they suck blood from human beings.

Human beings are a superior form of existence in comparison to mosquitoes, yet we are afraid of the tiny insects because they can pass around diseases such as brain inflammation, malaria, and polio.

I don't know how true it is, but some say that the demise of the ancient Hebrew nation and Roman Empire began with the onslaught of mosquitoes. Others talk about how the world's owl population is in danger of extinction because the owl chicks can't withstand mosquito attacks.

Sometimes, I question the Lord's wisdom in creating mosquitoes. In any case, I think they should all be sent to the moon, and flies, too.

During the country's poverty-stricken days many years ago, bedbugs and fleas were commonplace in our lives. They began to disappear as the country's economy improved. Some say that DDT (brought by the Americans during the Korean War) was responsible for eliminating these pests, or maybe the air pollution.

Mosquitoes are still with us, though, and I wonder how they managed to survive.

There used to be a shantytown behind the court building in Seosomun before the break of the Korean War. My elementary school was near there and every day after school my friends and I walked home by the ancient walls of Duksoo Palace. It was early afternoon and we always saw a Chinese woman who squatted down in the sun, catching and killing lice in her hair. As kids, we were fascinated and watched her, but she didn't seem to mind us at all. She'd go on picking the lice out of her hair with her fingers and crunch them between her teeth. That was many, many years ago, and the woman has long passed on undoubtedly, but her image is still vivid in my mind.

I remember telling my mother about the woman, and my mother would scold me, even spanking me for going so close to the lice-ridden woman. My mother would take out a fine-tooth comb and comb my hair very carefully then, afraid that I might have caught the lice from the filthy woman.

Lice have disappeared from our lives now, but mosquitoes still thrive. I was very surprised to see a big fat mosquito in Vienna, Austria, where my daughter was going to school. It was big and clumsy, and I caught it with my hand, which was rather different from the mosquitoes I was accustomed to. Mosquitoes usually reacted to the slightest movement and flew away.

Also, it seems that modern mosquitoes are more daring. They attack first, sit on my skin softly with their legs lowered, and ready to sting me. When I try to slap it, it slips out between my fingers and flies away quickly. I am left scratching where it has bitten me.

The mosquitoes used to disappear in the fall. Not any more. They are around all season long now and torment people like fleas had at one time. Sometimes, I see mosquitoes in my room well into the winter season.

My children are deathly afraid of mosquitoes and they burn a mosquito punk that look like spiral antenna in their room. It was a device that only the noble class could afford long time ago. But it is cheap and common now, and I suppose we're lucky that the device is readily available.

I smell the burning mosquito punk from the children's room and I recall my carefree days when I used to sleep outdoors counting the stars and listening to nighttime critters with a bonfire burning near me in the countryside village where I grew up. I haven't heard grass critter cry in a long while, ever since I moved to the city.

Now I fall asleep listening to the street noise outside. At times, I feel nostalgic for countryside sounds, even welcoming the thin, sharp noise of a mosquito that resembles the E string of a violin.

One night, I woke up to a whining high-pitched sound. I recognized the sound instantly, a sound that didn't belong to the cars racing by outside. I was reminded of a poem written by Lee In-row, a famous poet from the Goryo dynasty: "What an unlucky mosquito that you are for having to sit on my old skin through my rag of a shirt, instead of choosing a healthy body."

The mosquito's whine sounded like a crying baby looking for its mother. I felt sorry for it, even though I knew that it was looking for blood and protein it needed for laying eggs. And like the poet, I was ready to donate a drop of my old blood.

My arm was itching, which meant that I had already donated a drop of blood, though unwittingly. And another itch. I turned on the light and I saw a mosquito with its fat stomach stuck to the wall, looking very satisfied. My arm was already swollen red with multiple bites and my nail marks from scratching.

My sympathy for the mosquito disappeared suddenly, feeling only anger. I stretched my arm and slapped hard on it. I looked at my hand and I saw a red splash of my blood. I felt neither guilty nor sorry for having killed a living creature. Rather, I felt satisfied that I revenged the mosquito for its incessant attack on me.

As I have said, I was willing to give up a drop of blood for it to take me back to my nostalgic past even for a brief moment, but the reality of the mosquito's greed changed all that.

I cannot have it both ways, even though I had tried to do exactly that throughout my life in dealing with the people and the world around me. The simple truth is that the mosquito had pushed me too far, and I failed myself—and my belief—that we should respect all forms of life.

The mosquito incident leads me to wonder how well I have done with people, whether I have treated other people with proper respect. I am thinking that maybe I haven't.

This essay is reprinted from Korean Literature Today (Vol.11 No.1, Spring-Summer 2006)

All I Did Was To Sing

Songs, songs, songs. New-age songs blare out everywhere, radio, streets, and cars. They sound like noise: their rhythm is too fast; the words don't make sense. I try to give the songs benefit of doubt, though, and pay close attention to them. After a bit of trying, I understand the words and I sympathize with what the youth is saying and I try to sing along as I stomp my feet up and down. My aged body can't keep up with the music and I give up singing and dancing. Singing songs of the youth will not bring back my youth, but I try to recall the way I used to feel during my younger days, which was a long, long time ago. Something inside me tells me that I belong to a different era and I change the radio station to find slower music that I am familiar with.

There's a lot to be said for slow music. Moocho is a bean-family plant that thrives in the Winnan-seong region of China, and it is known to dance up and down to music. It responds better to slow rhythm than the fast pace.

When I was a child, my grandmother often asked me to sing in front of her visitors and friends. That was her way of giving me attention that she thought I needed as a fatherless child. As it turned out, I sang much better when I was alone and I froze stiff in front of an audience of any kind, disappointing my grandmother to no end. Till this day, I feel bad for my grandmother who had so wanted see me sing away in front of her friends.

I was not bashful about my singing forever, though. I recall my elementary school days, when the Korean War broke out. I was a fifth grader then and I had no idea what war was about. I saw the war as nothing more than a school outing. North Korean soldiers came, and many of our neighbors fled, afraid that the soldiers would rape and pillage like the rumors going around at that time.

My mother wasn't afraid, though. She stayed put with her two small children and she turned out to be correct in her assessment that we would be left alone. The northern soldiers were big on singing. At school, young men wearing red armbands played drums and taught us songs. Our homeroom teacher was not there, and we sang the songs at the top of our lungs. I didn't know what the songs meant at the time, something about communism and the great general named Kim Il-sung.

I have long forgotten the song titles, but I still recall the quick melody to words like "Ah, General Kim Il-sung, the name that shines bright..." and "Take the red flag and raise it high..."

Some time later, our soldiers and the UN troops returned to our neighborhood. I recall my mother smiling and breathing a sigh of relief. Seeing her smile, I felt like singing all of a sudden. I went out by the main gate and started singing "Ah, General Kim Il-sung, the name that shines bright..."

Then my mother ran out of the house barefooted and put her hand over my mouth and dragged me inside. She admonished me, "Don't you know that the world has changed now?"

I was puzzled then. My mother had become frantic for reasons I didn't understand. All I did was to sing a song. It wasn't until many years later that I understood what the war was about, an armed struggle between communism and democracy among the same people, brothers and sisters. Little did I know that the song praised the enemy general and that I shouldn't sing it.

The war was over in 1953 and in the 1960s I was into a different kind of songs, singing popular songs without much difficulty. I would hear a song blaring aloud outside a music store and memorize it. Then I sang the song all day until my family put their hands on their ears and pleaded with me to stop singing. I couldn't stop it, though. I continued to hum the song to myself until I mastered the song to my satisfaction.

Many years later, I ran a sweater manufacturing company. With over two hundred young loom operators weaving sweaters, someone would start singing. Soon the rest of the workers joined in, and the factory became a concert hall. Everyone forgot about the steaming heat as they sang to the rhythm of the machines. That was when I appreciated the power of singing, how songs can move people.

I think about the songs I used to sing as a youngster during the war and I understand now why the northern soldiers had taught me those songs. I also understand that I could have gotten my mother and myself into a lot of trouble with the southern authorities, had they caught me singing the praises of the northern general. Youngsters today sing different kind of songs, nothing to do with ideology or politics, and I think the world has changed for the better. I just wish that I could understand what they're saying.

Four Apologies to Mother

Blue House

My brother lives in America and he comes to visit us now and then. As his visit approaches, my mother turns into a different person, a woman waiting for her long lost love. Her love for her son is absolute, more so than she has ever shown for me or my husband. She never stays at my house for very long. When she does, she always talks about my brother, her pride and joy, in front of my husband. Once I asked her, "When was the happiest time of your life?" She replied right away, "When we three used to live together." I recall the way my mother used to send my brother and me off to school every morning and stand by the gate and watch us until she couldn't see us any more. Looking back, I think those were the happiest times for me, too.

She was overjoyed when my brother and I asked her to travel together this year, just the three of us. We decided to drive out to Yong Pyong, a resort town in Gangwon Province. My mother said to herself, "This is wonderful!" as she got into the car. My brother took the steering wheel whistling like a child. It had been a long while since he had gone on an outing in Korea.

The drive to Yong Pyong was long and hot. We arrived there after three hours in the near-hundred-degree heat, and the trip took a toll on my mother who was in her eighties. She lay down on her bed the minute we walked in the door.

No sooner did we unload our bags, my cellular phone rang. The caller said that the First Lady had invited the writers from Ewha University to the Blue House.

The Blue House! I was excited about visiting the presidential mansion. How often do I get to visit the Blue House, I said, and I accepted the invitation straight away.

I thought that my mother would be proud of the fact that her daughter was invited to the Blue House and that she wouldn't object to my acceptance. She didn't say a word as we turned around and headed back home.

The Blue House was truly magnificent, but it was a disappointing affair. We stood in the long reception line for a cursory introduction to the First Lady, had tea with pastries, listened to the remarks by the First Lady, took a group photo, and parted. Reflecting on what was to be the once-in-a-lifetime event for me, I thought I should have stayed in Yong Pyong with my mother and brother. I am sorry that I had to cut short our outing and make my elderly mother ride back with me in the blistering heat for nothing.

A Present for Mother

That year, I wanted to buy a major present for my mother. I opened a savings account for her present and made monthly deposits with the money I set aside from the grocery budget. I cut corners when I prepared meals and snacks, and sometimes I felt guilty for the shabby dinners that I made for my husband. It took forever to save enough money in the account.

When I asked my mother what she wanted, she replied without

hesitation, "Mink shawl." She shocked me with her answer. Her frugality was legendary, and I never imagined that she would ask for a mink shawl. Yet I was pleased that she knew what she wanted; I didn't have to spend a long time looking for a present for her.

She was happy and proud that I would buy a mink shawl for her. I still remember the pleased look on her face.

I waited for the day when she'd wear the shawl and show it off to everyone and say, "Look at what my daughter bought for me." Days and weeks went by, but she still hadn't worn the shawl, nor had she told anyone about the shawl.

Whenever I asked her why she didn't wear the shawl, she did not respond to me at all. This went on for a few years and one day, I happened to open her closet and found her shawl in a box. I opened the box to see that the once bright gray shawl had lost its luster and it looked awful. I lifted the shawl out of the box, and to my horror, the strands of mink fur fell off and floated down to the floor helplessly.

I understood then why she hadn't worn the shawl. The shawl was defective, yet she didn't have the heart to tell me there was something wrong with it. I tried to imagine what had gone through her mind all that time—whether she thought that I had bought her a cheap mink shawl. She should have said something, but she didn't. Was she afraid that she might appear ungrateful? By not saying anything, was she trying to spare me from disappointment? Or she simply couldn't bring herself to enjoy the bit of luxury she deserved. She has been tightfisted all her life, and old habits were hard to break, perhaps. Whatever the case, she had kept the problem to herself and struggled with it alone. Worse yet, she had not put any mothballs in the box, ruining the shawl beyond remedy. A mink shawl never looked the same to me ever since.

My Friend's Mother

My best friend whom I hadn't seen for twenty years came to see me with her mother from the United States. I used to like her mother as much as my own. As a youngster, I was always hungry and I used to pester her to buy me snacks, and she used to give me some money and tell me to study hard after these snacks.

My friend and I would make a beeline for a bakery or a Chinese noodle shop, forgetting about our promise to study. My friend's mother was warm and kind.

My mother, on the other hand, was very strict with my brother and me. Being a widow, she felt that she had to double her role as a father and a disciplinarian for us.

Parents Day fell in the middle of their visit, and we decided to treat our mothers to a trip to Jeju Island. I thought about staying at my sister-in-law's house there, but I booked us into a first-rate hotel for a night with a beautiful seascape for us to catch up on all those years.

I came out after making the reservation and saw my mother frowning. She was unhappy that I was wasting money booking two rooms. She insisted that one room was sufficient for four women. She also did not understand why I paid for the entire hotel bill. I explained to her that my friend would return in kind when I visit my friend in the United States, but she was not satisfied.

We ended up using just one room for all of us. My friend and her mother took the bed, which might as well have been a bed of needles for them. The atmosphere was so tense that they didn't get any sleep. My mother and I were crunched up together on the couch. I finally complained to my mother, "What good has all penny-pinching done for you so far? What good is the shawl that rots in the box?"

She couldn't sleep on account of her heart condition. But I turned my back to her and ignored her.

Literary Debut

Today I celebrate my literary debut. I had invited my mother and my brother for the occasion. All dressed and ready, my mother showed up at my house early. I gave my mother a couple of tips in etiquette for the gathering. I reminded her that she should chew quietly at dinner and that she needn't to eat everything off her plate as if she was cleaning it. Her expression turned dark momentarily when I told her this, but she did not seem offended.

We went to the gathering, and the ceremony began with Yeon Gu Park's congratulatory remarks for my literary debut including his generous critiquing of my writing. I made my customary reply, followed by a luncheon. I saw my mother seated in the front having lunch like mother queen and I felt proud. She looked pleased.

All of a sudden, the master of ceremony asked my mother to sing a song. I hadn't expected this and I became tense. My mother took the microphone without hesitation and began singing as if she had been waiting for the chance to show off her singing talent. In a voice of a soprano she sang, "Sanhong! How dare you go away without me! The world without you is a desert without water, a field without the moon, a harbor without lights."

I was fine up to this point, but she kept on. "Love turned cold, happiness gone, why did you abandon me..."

I could not bear it any more and I tugged at her dress signaling her to stop. But she ignored me and just moved on to the third verse, wailing words of a woman at her lover's gravesite.

I was so embarrassed and I wanted to hide. But my colleagues praised her singing and asked her to write the lyrics for them.

Afterwards, I complained to her, "How could you do that to me, singing a song like that?" Mother beamed a smile and took the bouquet of flowers I was holding. I had never seen her so happy.

Several years later, I heard from other people what my mother had told them. She told them, "I felt like my mission as a mother was completed at my daughter's literary debut." My mother is sick in bed now, waiting out her final days without any hope or mission, unable to recognize her own daughter.

In Vienna, Austria

This is my third trip to Austria. One might consider me extravagant for coming to Europe so frequently. I come to Europe to see my daughter who is going to school here in Vienna. She needs me, especially when she is preparing for examinations. I can't help her with the exams, but she says that she feels relaxed and comfortable with me around.

When I am with her, I forget about Seoul. But soon, I worry about the rest of the family back home, how they're getting along without me. Today I went out and rode on the subway to forget about Seoul and tour around Vienna. Vienna had fewer lines than Seoul, but the subway was less crowded. Some people brought their dog aboard and others baby carriages, which made for a peaceful picture.

Six years ago, I was a stranger filled with trepidation in this town, and I didn't dare to venture out to see the famous Stephen Pleats Cathedral and the Opera House. I was depressed, as gray as the sky.

But today, I felt as bubbly as a teenage girl on a journey as I got off the subway at the Calz Pleats station downtown. As I walked through the underpass, many wondrous sights caught my eye. People milling about without a care, a man with a dragon tattoo that was ready to fly off his shoulder and wrap around his neck and soar up to the sky, and a woman with a black rose tattooed on her chest snuggling against her man. The faint black rose appeared as if it was ready to bloom. I felt the excitement of the foreign land then.

Then I walked by some drug addicts with their eyes glazed over. They didn't look ashamed about their defeated lives. They seemed to have lost their thoughts, feelings, and past memories. On the other hand, a different set of crowd fill the Pavarotti concert in the opera house above the passage.

The bums didn't harm me, but I was afraid to walk near them. The minute I got away from there, all my fears melted away and I started thinking about their struggles. Their murky stares seemed to see through my materialistic greed and tell me that nothing in this world means anything.

I sat on a park bench on my way back. A man over seventy years old sat on the bench across from me. We sat in our respective benches without saying anything for a long time. I wondered what was going through his mind. Neither one of us said anything, and I wondered how the two of us could sit there without a word for such a long time. Was it the difference of skin color that prevented us from exchanging greetings? If we were in Seoul, he would have come over and asked me why I was sitting by myself, I was thinking. I missed the crowded city of Seoul then. The people here weren't that friendly, I thought. But then there are friendly people here, too. I'd asked them for directions, and they would go out of their way to show me the way.

There was a parliamentary election on October 3rd. The Nationalist Party pledged that they would grant 2,200 shilling— sthree times as much money as the ruling party was offering—for women who gave birth. They have a declining birthrate, and the

European women seem to view marriage and children as a sacrifice. If I were a citizen of this country, I wouldn't have to work for a living.

The other day I was invited to a concert by a Korean student studying here. I had to change trains a couple of times to get to the concert. The concert was crowded with many students from Korea and my friends from church, the preacher and his wife. I was so happy to see my fellow countrymen here in Vienna.

The concert began and the pianist entered the stage with the spotlight following her. She played pieces from Bach, Schumann, Mozart, and Beethoven, a fine performance beyond my expectations. I felt proud of her and the fact that she was a fellow Korean.

A small reception followed. There, I learned that her landlord sponsored the concert. He took the money that had been slated for his sixtieth birthday party and paid the expenses for the concert. I was touched by his generosity. I would have never given up my own sixtieth birthday no matter how talented the pianist might have been.

I watched the landlord and his wife congratulate the young woman and I thought that he seemed like her father rather than her landlord. In a way, he had the best birthday party he could have. It was a wonderful day in Vienna.

Work of Love

"Mom, I want to continue my studies." My daughter said when I arrived in Vienna yesterday.

I had a sinking feeling but didn't say anything. I thought that I had done my job as a parent by seeing her through her college graduation. I was hoping that she would get married and go on with her life now. She wanted to go on with her schooling, causing me to revise my thoughts.

My first impression of her living quarters was not a good one. Her room was shabby—her door barely hanging on hinges, the torn carpet, and the sponges trying to bust through the worn cushions on her couch. I couldn't understand why she wanted to continue with this life. She was lucky to get the room according to her. She got the room through the previous occupant who was also a Korean music student and had moved on to a prestigious music school.

My daughter has set her sights on the same school, ready to compete for the few open spots with young musical talents from all over the world. The life of a student in the foreign country wasn't going to be easy, not to mention the expensive tuition.

My daughter went off to her language class early this morning. I stand by the window and look out to see a woman about my daughter's age. She is calling after her child riding a tricycle around the street. It is a peaceful scene, and I think that she is fortunate. Happiness comes in simple things.

Below the window, a tiny plant with a yellow flower sways in the breeze. The flower has four petals and it reminds me of the four strings from my daughter's violin when she started to play the instrument.

She became interested in music the first day at her elementary school during the music recital by the school band. She wanted to play in the band just like the older kids, and my husband wasn't crazy about her new interest. He said that there was no precedent for musical talent in the family, and that pursuing music would take too much effort as well as money. I thought that we could afford her lessons if she wanted to pursue music, yet I wanted her to become a happy housewife later on in life.

But I couldn't persuade her to follow my wishes for her. I didn't think I should force my views on her either. So she began her lessons and she thrived. On bus rides to her lessons, she'd practice her fingering against her side, attracting attention from other bus riders. People thought she was quite something, and so did I.

The renowned violinist Chung Kyung Hwa's mother said that all she did was to pay close attention to her child and what she was saying. Who was I to tell my daughter stop playing her violin?

If anyone asked me whom I admired the most, I would name Thomas Edison's mother. Young Thomas Edison had his teacher baffled when he answered that one plus one equals one. His teacher told his mother that young Edison was retarded. She was not disappointed, however.

My daughter continued her music lessons with no sign of quitting. I was hoping that she would get tired of it.

I was an avid fan of classical music in my youth and I frequented music halls around Chongno area. I was immersed in the music, thinking that the music was written just for me.

My daughter was ready to graduate from the elementary school, and it was time to decide whether we should send her to an expensive art school or a regular middle school. We were struggling financially at this time, and my husband asked me to convince our daughter to give up her music.

I took her to the park on the Han River. Sitting by the shore, we tossed rocks at the river while I tried to make light jokes. I couldn't bring myself to tell her to give up her violin. She sensed that I was up to something and she remained silent. There is nothing more challenging than rearing children, and I had four of them to think about.

A friend of mine picked up on my dilemma and volunteered her advice. She simply said that I would be wrong to interfere with my daughter's destiny and that I would cause her resent me for the rest of her life. My friend said this without considering our dire situation financially, but she made me realize that I was blessed to have a daughter who wanted pursue her interest.

In the meantime, my daughter took the entrance exam to the art school and passed. We let her have her way and wished the best for her. Then my husband's business suffered a downturn. My daughter, sensing the deteriorating situation, began to falter in her studies. Her practices were becoming few and far in between, and I had to nag her to practice her violin, which was an odd switch of roles. At times, I wished that my husband had objected more strongly to her music school. Yet, my hopes for her grew and I persisted.

I am mending her frayed seat cushion as I listen to her play Beethoven No. 1 in D Major, one of the pieces she is going to play for the upcoming audition. The music starts soft like flowing water then reverberates louder and faster, alternating between ecstasy and despair of life.

I never expected that she would become a great musician but she far exceeded whatever the expectations I had of her. I feel smug. I have done my duty as a mother.

She finishes and smiles, satisfied. She says she feels good. If she doesn't pass the audition this year, she will stay and try again next year.

I stare at her, not sure how to take her remark. All I can think of is—how am I going to pay for another year for her? She looks determined, and I believe her. Raising children is work of love, to be sure, yet I wonder if it's a payback from my former life.

Man with a Flower

My husband who never brings even one bag of cookies for our children came home one day holding a pot of flowers in his hand. He wasn't the same person I knew, because he told me that he had picked it up at a flower shop on his way home. Well, I had never seen a flower like that before. It had two stems—one taller than the other—with five blossoms on top, no leaves.

I asked him what the flower was called, and he didn't know its name. "Why don't we name it ourselves? We can call it man-and-woman flower." I supposed that the two stems reminded him of us. His mind worked that way: he was the tall one and I was the short one. That was how he saw us together, even though we have lived together for forty years, which is long enough time for us to become equals.

We put the flowerpot next to the TV by the dining table, and often, the flower became a topic of conversation. It did very well, growing fast. I could tell the difference in growth from one day to the next. It also moved. During the day, the stems stayed apart with space in between. Come nighttime, though, the stems moved towards each other so close that I couldn't to tell them apart.

One day, I was up earlier than usual. The window by the dining table was turning lighter. I checked the flower like I do every morning, and I couldn't believe what I saw. Five flowers were in full bloom on top of the woman stem, looking down on the man stem. How was it possible that the stems switched places, I thought? The woman stood taller than the man, much like the phenomenon that occurred in an old marriage.

My daughter and I clamored that the stems switched places, but my husband ignored us. He merely said that the flowers looked like morning glory. I said that the flowers looked like lotus flowers, and my daughter thought they looked like lilies. They were light pink to begin with, and took on a reddish tone like baby's cheeks.

What is marriage? A man meets a woman, produces children, and the children repeat the process. God made Adam and produced Eve from one of Adam's ribs, thus the first couple. As such, a man and a woman are supposed to live in harmony without fighting. But then, show me a wife who never has packed her bags.

I have heard of a couple who have never quarreled, a while back. It is hard to fathom that there is such a couple in this world. Even if they existed, I don't envy them. I rather think that they are leading a boring life together.

There is an old saying that a quarrel between husband and wife is like slicing water with a knife, implying that it is impossible to delineate what and why they fight. There is a Japanese proverb "Nobody pays attention to the quarrel between husband and wife, not even dogs," meaning that these quarrels are very common.

I don't know why my husband and I fight. I have always thought of myself as a peacemaker, happy to cook and wash clothes for the family. Reflecting back, though, I've had many bitter moments, and I think I was trying to assert myself as an equal partner in life, family affairs, children's education, and so on. Sometimes I watch soap operas on TV and relate to the scenes involving family squabbles.

But then I feel very comfortable these days, perhaps accustomed to my supportive role in the family. I sense that my husband the head of the household is lonely and I know that I don't have the drive to lead. I sympathize with those in the leadership position and I like offering my wisdom in an objective way, but I don't want to be responsible. These days, we hear of women who are so aggressive as to beat their husbands. I don't understand these women, and I don't want to be one of them. I just want my husband to bring flowers home now and then.

Dear Mother, 1

When we said goodbye at the airport, I didn't cry, mother. I was all right as I watched you disappear behind the gate, that was, until I started to drive back home, when I felt my heart ready to burst. I was stuck behind traffic, but I didn't care. I wished that I were stuck in traffic forever.

Now, I am home. I walk up to your room on the second floor and open the door. I can see you sitting up in your bed smiling bright like a child as you take the breakfast tray from me. I can see you, but you're not here.

It is so quiet and desolate now. I was taking care of you like you were my child, the same way you had taken care of me, making for an odd turnabout in our lives. Is this what Buddhists call transmigration?

I sit on your bed and recall our hours together here. I keep telling myself that I should have done better, more than I had done for you. But then, we couldn't have gone anywhere together or anything like that because you were confined to your bed. I was just happy to have you here with me, even though tradition calls for you to be with your son rather than daughter.

Being traditional, you pined to be with your son and you waited for the day when you could join him. Today was the day, and there you were, disappearing behind the gate at the airport held up by my brother and his wife. I was heart-broken, but I was glad that you finally got your wish.

People around here didn't spare their envy when they found out that you were going to go to America to live with your son, but I knew that it wasn't important that you were going to America. You would have gone anywhere to be with your son.

Your friends don't come by here anymore. My second son has gone off to serve the military, and now, the house is empty.

As a young widow, you have done well to raise my brother and me by yourself. I wonder if you remember me asking, "You've had a hard life because of your children, haven't you?"

You didn't hesitate for a moment. You raised your frail arm and waved your hand and said, "Absolutely not..."

I choked back my tears, then.

Mother.

Like the old saying goes, a widower keeps three bushels of fleas in his house while a widow has three bushels of rice. And you were a rock for us two kids, working day and night and worrying about us incessantly until you turned eighty-four. You were a strict disciplinarian, harsher than any father around, and I thank you. You had prepared me for all the pains that were sure to follow as I grew up.

Everything has stopped for you now; only the curse of your disease and remorse remain. I watched you helplessly as you struggled to speak and all I could do was to curse the rotten fate and the useless medicine.

My friend tries to console me and say that one does well to live past eighty. Her words are empty. She can't know how I feel.

A late cold spell persists here in Seoul, exacerbating the void in my heart left by your absence.

Waiting for your visit in August,

Your daughter

Dear Mother, 2

Another year has gone by. It has been a long time since I saw you last, mother. I ask *oppa* how you are doing these days, and he replies weakly that your condition is deteriorating.

When you were near me I was disinterested in your welfare. Now that you are far away across the Pacific, I miss you terribly. I see the word mother in a book and tears well up in my eyes. My own children have left the nest now, and the house is quiet with no one to see my tears. I weep alone.

You were just twenty-four years old when you were left alone with two of us, which must have been a desperate situation for you. Yet I have nothing but fond memories from those days, and you made it so. Whenever I trace the happy memories, tears come at random as I walk down the street or sit in restaurants. People turn and look at me as if I were a mental case.

My children are grown up now, each with their own families. I had thought that I would find peace and quiet for myself, but I've become busier than ever. So I have no problem falling asleep usually. Today is different. Bits of memories rush at me tonight and I can't sleep. Outside, cold wind is shaking the window. And I think of the alleyway in Chung Jin. The moon was bright that night. You had just come out of the bathhouse carrying me on your back and you started singing in your beautiful voice. I didn't know what you were singing, only that I was happy and peaceful. Since then, whenever I run across difficulties, I revert back to that day in the moonlit alleyway, the warmth I had felt as I cuddled against your back.

But you weren't always a warm person. You sent me off to fetch water from the village well on freezing days. That was your way to make me a tough person, but I didn't see it the same way. I felt hurt when you forgot my birthdays, and for a long time, I was convinced that you were a mean mother. This impression stayed with me even after I got married and moved out of the house, and when you told me how much you missed me, I couldn't bring myself to believe you then. I doubted you and I regret my immaturity.

It has been five years since you left for America. I thought you'd be back here by now, but you are not here. Please recover from your stroke quickly and come back to me. I can't bear the thought of losing you in a land so far away from home.

The dawn comes, and my memories sink into oblivion. What remains is my longing for you. I miss you more everyday now. I want to tell you not to worry about me any more. You have made me a proud person like you and you should take comfort in your achievement. Just concentrate on getting well and come back to your daughter once more.

Invisible Mountain

I used to attend a number of gatherings regularly. I had led a busy social life with neighbors, mother's groups for my four children, and my husband's alumni group. Recently I have stopped all my social activities. It is because I feel guilty, ashamed that I have lost my daughter to the other world. She had been married barely one year when she died. Many people tried to console me with kind words, but they weren't much help. I reeled with a sense of guilt and I decided to stop talking to anyone.

The worst thing that can happen to a parent is to lose a child. I never imagined that such tragedy would happen to me and I have difficulty in believing it. All my years of trying to live as a magnanimous person were for naught, I felt.

My guilt is rooted in the fact that she never got to enjoy her life. I am thinking that she got the worst end of the stick during our poverty-stricken days. I recall the look of envy on her face as her friends were enjoying ice-cream on a stick. I can see her brooding in the corner of her kindergarten class when the other kids teased her about her school bag, the one I had made for her because I couldn't afford to buy one at the store.

She is always on my mind. Once at a gathering I addressed the person next to me by using my daughter's name, startling her. Another good friend tried to tell me that I would forget about it eventually, ten years at the most, and that people live on with worse tragedies. I think she is in heaven and I hope to join her there someday. I fear that I won't make it to heaven and never get to see her again.

I sit alone in the empty house, quiet with no trace of all the bustling that used to make me dizzy. It wasn't too long ago that I wished I could get away from all the chores, bringing dinners for my husband at his factory and coming home afterwards to look after our four children. I craved solitude then and I envied those lofty individuals who appear to enjoy peace and quiet and their intellectual pursuits. The French philosopher Michel de Montaigne once said that a life of solitude had its purpose in pursuing freedom.

Now that I have what I wished for, I struggle with the pain of loneliness rather than the spiritual freedom. I pursue only fractured bits of memory of my departed daughter and the pain that comes with them.

Tears come freely, and I am reminded of an old saying, "When you lose your husband, you lose the sight of the distant mountains; when you lose your child, you can't see the mountain in front of your eyes." My relatives who used to console me no longer mention her name. My own memory of her begins to fade, brewing new angst on top of the old. I look through her pictures and handwritten notes, trying to revive her in my mind. I am alone even in crowded subway trains. I find myself gawking at women about the same age as my daughter, so beautiful they look. After I am gone, will anyone remember my daughter the way I do? Will anyone care about her? I worry about that.

A deserted island may look lonely but no island stays deserted forever. There's always hope for the deserted island that someone will land there someday. Besides, the deserted island has seagulls and passerby ships for company. I have no such hope; she will never come back to me.

The loneliness I feel now is reminiscent of the loneliness I used to feel as a youngster waiting for my mother to come home from work every evening. I'd sit on the drum in the middle of the courtyard, my eyes trained on the alleyway in front of the house. I think I learned about loneliness there. Now, I miss those lonely days, when I had someone to wait for.

My daughter, too, used to wait for me to come home from work every evening. By a stroke of fate, mothers have passed on loneliness to daughters in our family. And oddly enough, we remain connected by the loneliness.

It's quiet outside tonight. I am not expecting any visitors. Yet I have a strange feeling that she might barge in any moment, calling after me.

A Black and White Photo

The television is showing a special on Korean War, and I'm glued to the TV screen flashing scenes from the war. The scenes evoke memories that have been dormant in me for a long time. In one scene, a girl is wailing in front of her mother's corpse, and in another, a boy is begging for milk for his baby sister.

These scenes remind me of myself during the war. My children seated next to me watch the TV screen, but they don't feel the tragedy of the war; they merely accept the fact that there was a war long time ago. I don't expect them to relate to the war the way I do; they hadn't experienced it themselves.

I like taking pictures, although I haven't taken new ones lately. The stage of life I'm in, I feel that I have spent most of the time allotted for me on this earth, with little left to go. I don't need to take new pictures. I sort out the pictures I have taken over the years, pondering which ones I should leave behind for my children. My children would remember me for sure, but after I am gone, there is no telling what they would remember about me. All these photographs will be no use to me then.

Though there is one picture I want to leave behind for them. It is black-and-white and was taken a long time ago. In the background, flags of many nations flap in the wind. An American reporter about sixty years old is holding a camera in one hand and a UN flag in the other. He is looking at a scraggly little girl standing next to him. I can't believe that the little girl in the picture is me, gaunt and shabby.

The picture represents many years of dire hardship ever since

my father died. My mother was mere twenty-four years old then strapped down with two children, my older brother and me. Being a sickly child, I used to wake up often at night and see my mother sitting up alone on the moonlit veranda. I didn't know what was going through her mind then, but remarrying was an option she had to have been contemplating because of the poverty-stricken condition we were in.

During the wartime, we didn't know when the next meal was coming or even if there would be a next meal. We endured many hungry days. One time, my mother had an idea to make flags and sell them to the troops of many participating nations. She sat up days and nights at her sewing machine and made flags and piled them up in the room. It was up to my brother and me to sell them. My brother took a box of them to Chong-no Street, and I went out to the bombed-out area near South Gate. I hung the flags on a couple of posts, and soldiers came and bought them. I was a shy child and I wasn't very good at selling. I only knew a few words like "How much?" and "This is..." Some of them wanted to bargain and others saluted to their respective colors and paid what I asked for.

I was so happy when the sun went down and the quitting time came. I forgot everything about the hard day, looking forward to going home to my mother and my brother. My brother was always done early and he would come to meet me near Duksoo Palace. He would take my box of leftover flags and walk me home where my mother waited with a pot of *doenjang* stew for us. She would beam happily when she saw us, and I thought we were the most fortunate people on earth.

It was different times then. Children nowadays can't imagine what we had to do to survive. My brother and I sold flags and my friend across the way shined shoes. Another friend sold ice bars on streets. Sometimes I wonder what they are doing now. If they are alive, I am sure they would retrace those days the same way I doing with the black-and-white photo.

It rained hard yesterday. Today, the wind blows hard and chases away the clouds. I look at the picture, wondering what life is. I feel as though I have oared across a huge, wind-blown ocean.

Tears

My mother is paying me a rare visit. She is lying down in her room, pensive and quiet. She is no longer interested in her favorite TV dramas. She seems depressed about her life, maybe even dissatisfied with the way my brother and I treat her.

I had seen many broken down elderly people before, never giving thought to the fact that my own mother would require convalescence some day, as well. It was just a few days ago, and she was full of life just as she always has been, a busybody. And I thought that she would never change her ways.

The day she left the hospital, the doctor said that her speech and movements had deteriorated, but her thoughts and feelings were the same as they always had been. He added that I should pay attention to what she wanted and look after her needs and make her smile. One smile a day would help her recover, he said.

I heed to his advice and try to put a smile on her face. I take a spoon and hold it like a mike and sing her favorite popular song. She doesn't smile. She ignores me and goes to her room. I am lost. Her silence kills me. I would rather have her admonish me for all the wrongs I've done in the past.

Of all the tears mothers of the world have shed, my mother probably can claim the most of them. She was always crying, whether she was happy or sad. She wailed on the day when my brother got into the prestigious Seoul University. That was the way with her, and I will always associate her with her tears.

When I was a little girl, I used to wake up to the sound of her weeping. I would see her leaning against the window and sobbing quietly. Her face looked pale blue in the moonlight. I kept my eyes closed and pretended that I was asleep. I told myself then that I would turn her tears into smiles when I grew up. I was too young to know why she was crying—whether she was overburdened with two little ones, or she was lamenting her status as a widow.

Come morning though, she was fine. She showed no sign of the tears from the night before, as she prepared my lunch box. Her sobbing during the night affected me in such a way that I couldn't think of anything else all day long. At school, I watched other kids go on playfully instead of joining them in the fun.

Mother kept on crying during the night. When autumn came, she didn't bother to hide her tears any more. She even cried during the day, crouched in the corner of the veranda. I couldn't bear to see her cry and I hated to go home. I lingered around my empty classroom after all the kids have left. Why was she so sad? I'd never cry in front of my own children, I used to say.

I grew up, got married, and had my own children. I found myself resorting to tears when I faced difficulties just like mother used to. I understood why mother had cried so much then.

My mother doesn't cry any more. A few days ago, mother's brother came by for a visit. She stared at him for a long time without saying anything. Her mouth quivered, but no tears came. After he left, she turned to me and said weakly, "I have no more tears."

I do the crying, instead. Mother is scheduled to leave for my brother's home in America soon. I go to my room and get under the blanket. I throw the blanket over my face and start crying. My daughter walks in and tells me not to cry, her voice quivering.

Kitchen Story

The kitchen is the first place I see when I enter my house. At the same time, I expect to smell food cooking in the stove, but it is not so any more. My kitchen used to buzz with activity every day. Now that my children have gone off on their own, the kitchen is empty, too big for just the two of us.

One of my friends came by the other day and remarked, "Your house looks so clean and empty like newlywed's." She was referring to the simple table setting I had made just for my husband and me. She was envious of our easy life, and I saw her point. But a kitchen is only a kitchen when the pots are boiling and the steamy aroma swirls around the woman of the house wearing an apron.

In my childhood, whenever I visited my friend, I stopped in her kitchen first, where my friend's mother greeted me wiping her hands on her apron. Steam poured out of the shiny black rice pot. I don't remember my friend, but I recall the kitchen clearly.

I may sound greedy, but I want to find happiness in the children's laughter and the sounds and smells coming out of my kitchen. I wasn't attached to the kitchen to begin with. As a new bride, I was never crazy about cooking and doing laundry. In fact, I felt stifled in the kitchen and I always wanted to get out of there in search of myself.

Once I took a long walk by the railroad tracks by myself. I felt free in my own thoughts. The sun went down, and I found myself alone in the dark. I panicked. More than anything, I was worried about the dinner for my family. I couldn't believe that I would miss my kitchen of all things. Then I realized that I enjoyed cooking for them, nurturing them.

My mother taught me cooking early on, and she had me making breakfast for her before I went to school in the morning. I made dinner for her after school, also. As a result, my hands were a mess, and I resented her nonchalance about my well being. Now I understand what she was doing. She was preparing me for the inevitable function in my life as a woman.

Ultimately, a woman's existence is one of sacrifice, and I want to see a change in the perception of women. A woman worrying about her man's health is beautiful. Women should be proud of their role in the kitchen. Jackie Kennedy is said to have chosen various dinner plates depicting different children's stories. That was her way of enticing her husband John to eat more.

Cooking is an art according to a famous chef, and I agree wholeheartedly. The kitchen is a place to produce meals to be sure. For me it is also where life begins. I learned about life from my mother who persevered through her harsh conditions. She used her apron for cooking and for wiping her endless tears. She taught me about patience.

I tried to teach my own children the same values throughout our difficult times. We had many bad days. No matter how bad things were the day before, I found new energy the next morning as I prepared their breakfast and lunch boxes. The sounds and smell of the food I was cooking for them energized them. My cooking was never extravagant, though. In fact, I was trying to get out of our poverty by cutting back on groceries, and the children understood me. Sometimes, I look at their shortness in height and regret that I had overdone it. I try to tell myself that I hadn't shortchanged them in nourishment.

I recall the shabby rental in Chungmuro 4-ga we used to live in. I had an apple packing box for a kitchen cabinet and an outdoor charcoal grill for a stove near the outhouse. On rainy days, I had a tough time finding a dry spot for the stove and I wished for a kitchen with an eave so that I could cook under cover.

Now that I have a modern kitchen with all the latest technology, I feel a new kind of chill and I don't know why.

Family Emblem

I walk into the lobby of a big building and come across an exhibit of family mottoes. I read all of them carefully and I find them to be very appropriate. If everyone behaved according to these mottoes, this world would be a perfect place to live. Some people point to the disintegration of family values and say that it is the cause for the confusion in our society. I haven't heard of similar exhibits in other countries.

Every family has its traditional motto, and so does the society. Not many years ago, I used to see in public places like governmental offices and banks mottoes such as 'Honesty,'

'Diligence,' 'Integrity,' 'Patience,' 'Cooperation,' and 'Conciliation.' Pictures or paintings have replaced these calligraphic pieces now. I understand that the world is changing, yet I long for those unforgettable words that linger on like those of my mentor from old days. As a nation, we managed to get through the difficult times during the Japanese colonial rule and the unprecedented fratricide called the Korean War because of our ancestor's teachings, I think.

My youngest son had asked me to write our family motto for an exhibit at his middle school long time ago. I was not adept in calligraphy. I didn't know what to write either.

The only family motto my mother had drilled into me was: 'When you have the money... that is when you must be frugal.' I had no idea what she was talking about. I only knew that we were poor and I hated being poor. I saw my mother pick up spilled grains of rice and watched her fish out coins lodged in between floorboards. She used to say "Coins turn into big money," or "If you respect money... only then will money love you."

I didn't want to write, "When you have the money... that is when you must be frugal" for my son's school project. I feared that his classmates might tease my passive son. I was too proud to have my son associated with my poverty-stricken background. I wrote something loftier and gave it to my son. I don't remember what I had written then.

Even though I was ashamed of my background, I knew deep inside that my values were rooted in my mother's teaching. Her words helped me get out of poverty along the way. I should have been proud of my mother and her words. I should have been proud of the way I had overcome poverty.

I remember reading about the state of poverty in Germany after the Second World War. To save matches, they waited until there were three people before they lit a match. They talked proudly about surviving on "eintopf," a meal made of leftovers all boiled together.

I often ask myself why I couldn't have been so brave as to talk about and write my family motto for my son with pride. There is a saying that a daughter takes after her mother. Reflecting my own life, it seems that I have built a great distance between my mother and me.

Stress

A person with a chronic ailment gets no respect. I have been suffering ulcers for thirty years. I try not to show my pain, but sometimes my family catches me and asks me if I'm sick again. I feel bad for my husband for having married a sick woman. I console myself by saying that if there's going to be anyone sick in my house, let it be me, no one else in the family.

Ulcers can attack any time, even while I'm at a dinner table. I would be enjoying a meal along with everyone else, when suddenly I would lose my appetite for no reason. Once I read about an episode with Henry David Thoreau, the author of Walden. He was invited to a dinner. Seeing that the host was arrogant, Thoreau said that there was nothing for him to eat and left. I am not comparing myself to Thoreau; I am just saying that I understand how he felt. If I am feeling well, I can enjoy any food. If I am not feeling well, I cannot touch anything, even the best cuisine. At times like this, I think that some other organ controls me rather than my sense of taste. This may be one of those phenomena neither science nor the field of medicine can explain.

Some people refer to the human body as a miniature universe, much of it remaining unknown. Some experts say that stress is the basic reason for modern illnesses. If that is the case, I, too, must be under tremendous stress. I am but a housewife without any major concerns other than cooking and washing. In that sense, my ulcer is a misplaced ailment that has stayed with me for the past thirty years.

In the Ladakh region of the Himalayas where it is free of

materialistic contamination, the villagers are said to consider angry people as most insulting. Anger has no place in their lives because it does little in resolving stress. I am aware that food should be enjoyed in order for it to do good for the body.

My problem for many years was that any little comment caused stress for me, and I couldn't eat. I checked into a hospital after many years of struggling with the pain. Looking out of the window, I saw trees and a wire fence surrounding the hospital. I felt separated from the outside world. Then I saw a ragtag bum leaning against the wire fence jamming a handful of food into his mouth. How I envied him then for his healthy appetite! He seemed so happy that he had a healthy stomach.

I was swallowing more pills than food then, feeling lost and lacking. I spent my days lamenting my hapless stomach. I began to hate my helper who ate a bowl of rice dowsed in hot bean paste and chewed loudly on hot chili pepper for lunch.

Another aspect of ulcers was that I never felt hungry. Loss of appetite meant a sign of hopelessness. I found myself longing for my days of youth, when I was always hungry. We were struggling to eat one meal a day then and I never had imagined that I would ever lose my appetite for food. But there I was — rejecting food even though I could afford to eat whatever and whenever I could. I would turn down invitations for a gathering on account of my ailment and I felt desolate and unhappy about my life.

At the hospital, I underwent a series of tests. The most difficult was the intestinal test. They injected white substance into my intestines and told me to bear the pain until they took pictures. It was a torture. All the tests completed, including the stomach test, I sat with my doctor face-to-face when the results came in. I felt more like sitting in front of a judge than a doctor, ready for my final verdict. I was tense.

The doctor pulled out various x-rays from a large yellow envelope and examined them against the lighted screen and said, "You are fine, there's nothing wrong with you." Then he asked me if I had experienced indigestion when I had tried to enjoy food by pretending that my bad memories were good memories. He added that I should try to fix the problem by nutritional methods rather than coming to the hospital.

I thanked him and walked out of his office. I thought about what he said about my memories. They were all painful ones, and I didn't want to recall them. I had thought all along that I was the only unhappy person in this unfair world.

The doctor's remarks changed my life. He made me realize that I must find some good out of my distressful and sad past. It wasn't easy to do.

What good was there in the failed clothing factory and all the struggles to pay off the debt? No one wanted to buy the factory, so we had to sell the building and discard all the equipment. We managed to pay off the debts and we felt thankful.

As fate would have it, my husband was involved in a catastrophic accident, resulting in major brain surgery. Our dismal future brightened when he managed to recover. It was a miracle. I had forgotten how happy I was. There was some good, after all. Whether a certain event was stressful or not was all in how you looked at things.

I decided to listen to my body instead of blaming my ancestors for giving me a bad digestive system. If I craved for something to eat, I stopped whatever I was doing and gave in to what my body wanted.

Fortunately, my body doesn't ask for a great deal. Soups, mostly. Wheat dough dumpling soup, soybean paste soup, cabbage soup, and such. I crave for ground fish soup, but it's rare.

I am happy to be able to make these for myself. If I could make food for myself till the day I die, I could wish for nothing more. I like fruits as a side dish, sometimes. I like the feeling of the freshness as I swallow the fruits.

One day, I was at a buffet ferrying back a plate with rice and watermelon. A passerby woman saw my plate and whispered to me, "The fruits are dessert."

I would have been annoyed by that remark in the past. Instead, I replied smiling, "Ah, I didn't know." I felt happy-go-lucky.

If I can't win the battle of stress, I am going to embrace stress and live happily together.

Life's Road

There is an axiom that the habits one acquires at age three last till eighty; but really, one's habits seem to change according to circumstances. In my younger days, I used to feel afraid of being alone. Now, I prefer being alone in quiet settings. In psychological terms, my preference for solitude could be construed as a sign of depression I suppose, but my condition may just be a natural occurrence that comes with age. I will reach my final station in life alone and leave this world by myself anyway. And it might not be a bad idea to prepare myself for the inevitable.

However, I do feel like going on a trip with a close friend of mine just to wander about here and there in the countryside, not necessarily overseas. But I don't think she or anyone elso would take time out of her busy schedule to cater to my sudden urge to travel. Besides, there's no guarantee that the trip would be fun for all concerned.

Still, I want to go off with a friend and find our way like we used to as children when we'd get lost. I would spit into one hand and slap my finger on the spit to see which way the spit splashed. That was the direction we'd follow. We would never get lost. There are roads everywhere, even in the sky, over the sea. All roads are connected—even the random animal tracks in the deep forest—and we'd never get lost.

Modern boulevards have their own appeal, straight and wide, but I prefer winding alleyways sometimes. The straight open roads are made for people who subscribe to reason and data as their guide in life, while the meandering alleyways without ends seem to accept everyone including wayward individuals.

I had such a winding road in mind as I went on an outing today. Driving thirty minutes or so outside Seoul, I found a small hill overlooking a meadow with wild flowers and I felt welcomed there. I sat down and looked up to see cotton clouds hovering in the blue sky. A hazy day moon hung over the mountain in the distance. It was the kind of place that you see in an ancient painting, houses with thatched roofs clustered together at the foothill of a mountain, while a thin layer of fog hovered over the river valley. The houses with thatched roofs have been replaced with modern homes, nestled in between a few commercial buildings. Still, the village looked quaint like a painting, preserving delicate harmony between the old and the new. I was so impressed by the scenery, I wondered if heaven would look like it. If I were to come to a place like this after I die, I thought to myself, I would have nothing to fear.

Nature has arranged that all living things must come to an end and the anticipation of this finality makes us afraid, not the death itself. One is said to feel peace and tranquility at the moment of death. Somewhere in a faraway island, I am told that the elderly choose death, come the right time. The elderly climb a tree and his or her family circle around the tree and sing.

Flowers bloom and fall.
Fruits ripen, fall to earth.
So must we.
We come and go.

For them, there's no place for sadness for either the departing or those who remain behind, only a song of celebration. They accept nature as it is given to them, and I feel humbled by their view on life.

I recall a proverb that says that one should look up at the sky once a day after reaching the age of fifty. I recall a Confucius saying, "I don't know about life yet, how would I know about death?"

Across the meadow in the distance, I could see the villagers move about idly. They looked tiny like ants, and I wondered what sort of lives they were leading. Who, among them, were going through life on a major thoroughfare and who were struggling? Everyone wants all the roads open to them and they want to choose the way best for them, but life isn't meant to be that way. In my case, I have to live with the pain from the loss of my daughter as well as sharing the difficulties my son had to endure. Life isn't meant to be fair.

The way to the holy land is through contemplation, imitation, and life's experience, they say. Contemplation is the ideal way to determine one's course of life, and imitation is the easiest. I had thought that life's experience was the best teacher of all, but it turned out to be the most difficult means.

We rush to get ahead in life, which tends to bring about disastrous results at times. I have been intensely focused on achieving success in life and nothing else. As a parent, my most important mission in life was to provide the best for my children.

Traditionally, parents claim success if their children pursue the same interests in life, but I don't even know what my children think of me. I ask my younger son about getting married, and he replies half-jokingly, "I am afraid that I'd end up with a difficult person like you, mom."

I had hung all of my hopes and dreams on my children and I wish I had done things differently. If I had to do it all over again, I would allow time to appreciate the flowers in the meadow and the clouds gliding along without a care in the world.

I look back on my life and all the hardships I had to endure to get here, the unrelenting nightmares. It seems that I have been on the grueling road forever. The end is within sight now, and I just hope to be remembered as a wildflower on a deserted path in the middle of a forest. That is not too much to ask, I am thinking. A couple of sparrows on the electric line overhead seem to read my mind. They jabber and rub themselves together as if they're laughing at my greedy wish.

Dancing with My In-law

Today, I am scheduled have lunch with my in-law, my daughter's mother-in-law, specifically. My daughter and her husband are too busy to visit with their respective parents, and I want to stay in touch with my in-laws at least. In staying close touch with them, I am thinking of my daughter's marriage and her happiness. Young people depend on their love for happiness nowadays, but passion cools in time, lasting no more than two and a half years on average. I would do well to maintain a harmonious relationship with her in-laws for the sake of my daughter's marriage and happiness. I had devoted thirty years to raising my daughter and I consider myself an expert on her habits and feelings.

In preparation of my own marriage, my mother had told me about the virtues of sacrificing myself and following my in-laws and their life style in blind faith. But I don't wish the same for my daughter. She would never listen to me anyway, not in this day and age when the entire world is accessible at the touch of computer keys. I had brought her into this world, but sometimes I am made to feel that I am responsible for her body only, not her soul.

Once in a while, I ask her questions about what she had done on certain things, and her eyes turn hard and narrow: *I'm not a little girl any more.* Nevertheless, she looks like a young girl to me, and I can't help but worry about how she will manage all the ups and downs of her life. Whenever she looks at me like that, I feel very distant from her, even though she is right in front of me.

There is an old saying—when two in-laws pass each other on a narrow levee in between rice paddies, the bride's parent takes the lower, wet side of the levee while the groom's parent stay on top. Worse yet, some ancient proverbs characterize the parents of a daughter as sinners, or afflicted, which I think exists only in our culture. Other cultures may share a similar notion, but no matter, it is unfair.

Several days ago, I got a strange telephone call near dawn. The caller didn't say a word. I could hear the caller breathing and I yelled "Hello, hello" into the receiver. Still, the caller didn't say anything. I never liked telephone calls late at night to begin with. The call about my husband's traffic accident had come late at night.

I hung up the telephone, full of apprehension. I couldn't get back to sleep, imagining the worst. *Was it my husband's secret lover that I hadn't known about? Or, was it my brother in America who called to tell me about mother's worsening condition, but didn't have a heart to go through with the call? Did my son and his wife have a fight? Did they decide to call it quits? Had my daughter have a quarrel with her husband and called me, only to realize how late it was and hung up?*

All these worries were groundless, I knew. So many bad things had occurred without any forewarning in my lifetime, and I couldn't stay calm.

I was about to call my children, but I changed my mind. I'd be waking them up in the middle of the night for nothing. They wouldn't understand my constant worries about our family affairs. I called my brother in America—where it was early evening—and asked him if mother was all right. He told me talk to her directly and put mother on the telephone. I had so much to say to her, but words wouldn't come out. She repeated, "I can't hear, I can't hear." I barely managed to say hello and hung up.

Having verified that my mother was all right, I turned my attention to my daughter. I was deathly curious about her wellbeing and I called my in-law and made an appointment to see her as soon as it was light.

It is best to keep distance from in-laws as an old saying goes. I am aware of the certain protocols that in-laws observe out of respect for each other. But I don't want to feel stymied by the traditional conventions. I feel bonded to my in-law, the woman who had entered my life through the marriage between her son and my daughter. It is no coincidence that we were brought together. Out of all the people in this world, my daughter had become her myonuri by a stroke of fate. Our children's matrimonial bond has made both of us grandmothers-in-waiting. Yet, I am cautious that our familiarity would breed contempt and invite undue harm to my daughter. I try to meet her face-to-face whenever I need to talk to her about something and vice versa.

We meet at a restaurant, talking animatedly about our respective families. Soon, I learn that my daughter and her husband had not quarreled; the blues I had felt earlier lift away. I am reinvigorated, so is she. We had finished our lunch long ago, but neither one of us are thinking about leaving. The waitress keeps looking at our way: *when are you leaving?*

I don't know who came up with the idea, but we decide to continue the conversation at her home, where she lives with our children. Why don't we just meet at my house next time and cook for ourselves so we don't have to worry about the restaurant people, she asks? That way, we save money and we can prepare dinner for our kids, too. We clap happily, what a great idea. I feel like dancing as I imagine the surprise our kids would walk into when they come home from work. What would they say when they see that both of their mothers had prepared dinner for them ... I don't finish my thought; my mah-eum is already there at their house, filled with anticipation.

We spot a farmer's market in front of a bank; it's a market day for Farmers Coop Bank. My in-law knows what her son likes and she goes ahead. I follow her. She picks a bundle of giant green onions, two pieces of radish, and three dried pollack fish. She ought to get more goodies to satisfy her thirty-four-year old son, I'm thinking. I don't say anything, though. She walks ahead of me carrying the plastic bag, her steps as light as a dancer.

We arrive at her house, and she unlocks the door. The air that had been locked up all day rushes at us. We walk in, and no sooner than we take off our jackets, she goes to the kitchen with the shopping bag, and I go to my daughter's room, holding a broom in my hand. We proceed to our respective stations without saying anything as if we had rehearsed the routine. I sweep and mop the young couple's room. She puts on the rice.

She hollers from the kitchen, "How shall I slice the radish?"

I reply, "You know, whichever way you like..." I have no preference.

She starts slicing, and I go on sweeping and mopping. No longer empty and quiet, the house fills with sounds of chopping, slicing, and dicing. We're getting ready for a huge celebration, not a simple dinner for two.

The pollack stew boils. We set the table and put the stew pot in the middle of the table and sit down. We smile at each other, satisfied. We pick out the meaty chunks from the center parts of the pollack fish and set them aside for the young couple for later. We take tailpieces and heads and put them in our own bowls and start in. It is a grand feast, matched by none. In my mind, a song lingers, a song about dried pollack fish.

> Dark blue sea, under the sea
> I roam in a school, drink icy sea
> until I grow big and fat,
> when
> I become dried snack for a poor poet
> drinking soju.
> That's fine with me, I say, better yet,
> I want to be his poem.
> He may strip off my flesh in bits'n pieces
> until it is all gone,
> nothing left but my name,
> myeong tae. (myeong, bright; tae, great)
> Ha ha ha ha.

Tree with a Ribbon

My sister-in-law sent me four boxes of tangerines. I was very touched. She had put in a lot of time and effort packing the fruit that she had grown herself in her ranch. Considering her age and weak health, it couldn't have been easy for her to work so hard under the hot sun throughout the summer, caring for each tangerine. I felt grateful, but with reservation. Knowing about the pain and the suffering she had gone through to produce the fruits precluded me from enjoying them freely. Besides, I thought, if I wanted tangerines, I could buy them at the store. Why did she go through all this trouble, sending me four boxes of them? It was with such ambivalence that I had received the gift. I was grateful, yet I wasn't sure how to thank her.

I called her and thanked her, anyway. She thanked me instead for accepting them. There was an overabundance of tangerines now, and most of them rot on the ground and go to waste.

Historically, Jeju tangerine was a rare commodity, reserved only for the royalty. King Mun Jong, for instance, had written a poem praising its delicacy:

Vegetables and their fragrance
may please my nose;
meats may satisfy my tongue.
Jeju tangerines please my nose
and my tongue simultaneously.
This is the reason for my love
for the tangerines from Jeju.

The popularity of the tangerines among the royal subjects prompted the government officials to institute an accounting system in order to keep track of the fruits. During the Goryo Dynasty, the officials swarmed the orchards to inventory and tag the fruit trees the day they started bearing fruit. They tagged each tree and recorded the number of the baby tangerines that hung on the tree's limbs. The grower was expected to harvest and deliver the same number of mature tangerines from the tree. Should the grower fall short of the number that was recorded on the tag, the local officials handed down severe punishments. The growers became disenchanted with the unfair policy that demanded production regardless of the conditions beyond their control, the weather, for example. There was no guarantee that every budding fruit would reach full maturity. The growers devised a way to beat the system. The only way to escape punishment was to kill off the trees. They made holes in the trees and filled the holes with pepper powder, killing them without being detected. The killing went on for years, and the tangerine trees became almost extinct.

It took many years to bring back Jeju tangerines. When I met my sister-in-law in Jeju for the first time some years ago, the tangerines were very valuable. She used say, "One tangerine tree will put my kids through college," and brag about her trees endlessly. I recall going out to her orchard that night. I stood in front of the tangerine trees under the moonlit sky and felt something holy about the trees. They had gone through so much and managed to survive.

The situation has changed now. When I went to visit her as recent as two years ago, her trees were weighed down with ripened tangerines. I asked her, "The tangerines are ripe. Why haven't you picked them?"

She replied, "It doesn't pay to pick them. It's cheaper to let them drop and rot and fertilize the ground."

Sure enough, I saw an elderly gentleman next door picking off the tangerines and letting them drop to the ground.

I was appalled.

The fruit's abundance doesn't make it valuable any more. Tangerines are piled up in stores all over the city, and people don't pay any attention to them. People take it for granted that the Jeju tangerine will always be there for them, the soft skin that you can peel away so easily, the sweet-yet-sour juice that squirts in your mouth as you sink your teeth into the soft meat.

I look at the tangerines my sister-in-law has sent. The fruit and its tumultuous past remind me of our own past as a nation of people. I take a handful of the tangerines into my bosom and walk over to my dining table and sit down.

Dancing with My Granddaughter

Young people nowadays laugh when I tell them how I got married. I didn't get to pick my lifetime partner. My mother had picked a husband for me. It was at a time when young people like me were beginning to think that the traditional brokered marriage belonged in the past, old fashioned.

I was never one to argue with my mother, though. Being a so-called mama's girl, I didn't know how to refuse her even as a teenager, when I was supposed to be full of resentment towards adults. I thought that any indication of disobedience on my part would destroy her, negating everything mother had done her entire life. So, when she began looking for a husband for me, I let her do what she had to do. She insisted that it was better for a young woman to get married as soon as possible and she got busy talking to elderly marriage brokers just as my college graduation approached.

She set a high standard for potential candidates, as if I were a Cleopatra or something. First of all, she didn't want to consider any first-born male because of the burden he would have to bear in carrying out the family's ancestral rituals forever. She was afraid that the responsibility would fall on my lap. Moreover, she determined that the potential groom had to be diligent, if not rich. It wasn't important that he had impressive academic credentials, but he had to be practical.

I, the bride, didn't have much to say about any of this. Our house was buzzing with activity, all the relatives and friends coming and going day and night. I could hear mother telling others how well she had trained me in etiquette and mannerism and so on.

Her sister came by one day with information on a boy. He was not a first-born, but third, and mother became excited even before she met him. After we met him together, she liked him a lot (much more than I did) and she went ahead and set a date for the wedding. I felt rushed during the process, and for this reason, I struggled through my days as a new bride. Whatever the sweetness a newlywed was supposed to experience, it didn't happen to me.

After we were married, my husband told me that he (therefore I) had the duty to perform *jesa*, the ancestral ritual for his family. I

couldn't believe it. I married a third son to avoid all the troubles of *jesa* but here I was, charged with preparing for the rituals for his clan, including all the food for the gathering.

I protested to my mother, but she wasn't interested in hearing me. She merely said that women were supposed to tend to *jesa*, and that was the end of the conversation, forgetting that she was the one who had insisted on a son without the burden of performing *jesa*.

I watched a TV program the other morning, featuring a married couple. The woman was ranting and raving, airing out all the grievances she had accumulated during her marriage. Her husband sat quietly all the while, listening to her tirade. I wondered, *doesn't she know that the nation is watching her? Did they get married on their own or through a marriage broker?*

The announcer asked, "If you had to do it all over again, would you marry your husband?"

The woman said no, waving her hand.

I asked myself the same question. I couldn't answer right away, but I concluded that I had done well to survive my marriage for forty-five years without too much complaint.

When my daughter turned old enough to get married, I wanted to find her a mate just as my mother had done for me. I wasn't sure if she would go along with the idea but I tried, anyway. I suggested cautiously, "My mother arranged a partner for me when I was your age and I have devoted myself to motherhood ever since. That's how I lived my life. How about you?"

Surprisingly, she wasn't opposed to the idea. She said it was all right for me to select and interview some candidates and she would make the final decision. We agreed on the plan and proceeded with the wedding.

After the wedding, however, her attitude was different. She said, "Women of your generation devoted themselves to motherhood, and that was your way. But I am going to raise my children and have a career as well."

I sympathized with her, although I thought that it would be a monumental task for her to raise a child and hold down a job at the same time. She persisted, however, and I couldn't stand by idly and watch her. My mother had ignored me while I was struggling with *jesa*, my second vocation. But I couldn't ignore my daughter the way my mother had.

I pick up my three-year-old granddaughter in the morning and drop her off at home in the evening. I do grocery shopping for my daughter sometimes as well. On days I want to take a rest, my cell phone rings indubitably. My daughter says frantically, "Mom, baby has a fever. Could you take her to her doctor?" Or, she says, "Mom, the deadline for the signup at the kindergarten is tomorrow."

My friend watches me running around with my granddaughter and says that I have a new "dance partner" as the new excitement in my life. I am not alone in this dance. At my granddaughter's kindergarten, I see more grandmothers than mothers looking after the children. I am reminded of an old saying—a parent's work is never done—and I smile.

Geum Gang (Diamond) Mountains

I have long imagined Geum Gang Mountains as a place where bent pines grow among unnamed plants and the winding paths along the brooks in deep gorges remain untouched by humans. Ancient songs depict the mountain using different names according to seasons, for there aren't enough words to describe its beauty. As a youngster, I had memorized a shijo poem about Gae Gol Mountain, which had left a profound impression on me. Visiting Gae Gol Mountain has been a life-long dream of mine, and I was ready to drop everything to see it whenever an opportunity arose.

The sixty years of political division between South Korea and North Korea had preempted any thought of visiting Geum Gang Mountains in the North. It was unthinkable for a South Korean like me to visit Geum Gang until recently, and so when the opportunity came, I grabbed it right away.

The day came, and I boarded the bus with great anticipation. We passed by a rusty sign marking the 38th Parallel and about 2 km later the bus stopped. Several Northern soldiers came aboard the bus, took a quick glance around the bus and got off without saying anything. Then the soldiers paired up in two's and marched away in high goose steps. I felt as though I was in a different world, despite the same faces and the same language. Outside the bus, the Hae Geum River flowed by nonchalantly, skirting around Gamabong Mountain. My mind wandered. What would the mountain's guardian spirit say about all the goings-on between the Hae Geum River and the Han River? I woke up from my trance and saw clouds floating by over the Gamasong Mountain, the same clouds I saw in the South.

The guide stood up and gave us detailed instructions on conduct. *Stay with the group. Refrain from talking to anyone. Be sure to use trashcans. Smoke in designated areas only. How to use toilette facilities, etc, etc. You must follow the rules, otherwise, you have to pay fines and face additional consequences.* The talk of fines and punishments sounded oppressive and didn't sit well with me, but I supposed that the rules were necessary to protect the pristine environment. When in Rome, you must do things the Roman way, I told myself and relaxed. *Do what they tell you, eat what they give you.*

It was the first time on northern soil since my childhood there were so many things I wanted to see and do other than visiting Geum Gang Mountains. But my schedule was preset by Hyundai and the North Korean government, to tour Geum Gang Mountains for three days.

Mahn Mul Sahng (mountain with ten thousand faces) and Hae Geum River (treasure by the sea) were on the menu the first day. It was raining, and our guide suggested that we limit the tour to Hae Geum by the sea and skip the trek up the mountains.

I protested and insisted on seeing Mahn Mul Sahng. When would I get another chance to see the Diamond Mountains? A little rain wasn't going to deter me from seeing the subjects of songs and poems. The guide relented, and we set out for Mahn Mul Sahng.

The monsoon rain that had arrived from the South showed no

sign of letting up. We donned rain gear, bunched up together bright yellow and white, like flowers. Ten minutes up the trail, the mountain's peak boulders revealed their shapes and disappeared behind the clouds. Strangely shaped rocks and boulders that nature had sculpted stood taciturn behind the foggy drizzle, signaling a mystic presence all around me. As I climbed, I evoked images of holy, righteous, people who had gone before me. I held the wet railing and felt their energy flowing through my hand, the power of forgiveness of sins buried deep inside me. A stream, together with the new rainwater, danced down the ravine to the right, pounding and swirling about the mighty rocks. Its sounds, its dignity had a humbling effect on me, and I took each step with reverence.

Meanwhile, I fell behind the group. I had been pacing myself from the start in the interest of conserving energy, and now, I struggled to stay up with everyone. I breathed hard, sweat pouring out of me like rain. The lofty thoughts had evaporated, and I focused on negotiating metal steps up the steep hill, crouched through small tunnels, then up the stone steps. A mistake here would be fatal.

Grasping for air, I asked the guide from the North, how much further? He replied, "We came two thirds of the way. Keep going." I couldn't turn back and I focused on the peak and kept moving ahead. I reached the peak finally. I had dreamt of being there for so long and I had made it.

I recalled a story about Grandmother Mandeok, not my real

grandmother but a legendary woman known for her great generosity. She had donated all her fortune to the people starving in Jeju during the seven-year drought. Hearing about her generosity, the King held a banquet in her honor and asked her what her wish was. She answered, "If I had one wish, I would like to see Geum Gang Mountains before I die, sire."

Standing at the peak, I looked out into the distance in search of the legendary rocks and boulders of ten thousand faces. The entire mountain range was covered under a sea of clouds. I couldn't distinguish the sky from the mountains. From there, I couldn't see any distinguishing marks between the North and the South. If the two ideologies came together like the clouds over the sky and the mountains... unification would be so simple. The clouds down below looked comfortable for me to sit on, and I thought that there must be a way to find love and peace underneath it.

The talk of unification had gone on for fifty years without any result. But if I could only return to Geum Gang Mountains after the unification... I would climb up to Biro Peak, the tallest peak of them all.

From far away, I heard a crow... as if to remind me of my old age.

Reason for Wind

It is November, time to get ready for winter. But it doesn't feel like winter is on its way. In the old days, I would have been frantic preparing for the winter this time of the year. I'd be shopping for cabbage for a year's worth of winter kimchi and coal briquette to keep warm during the winter months.

I go and do some chores around my apartment, nothing in particular. After a while, I stop my chores and look out the window and the street down below. Out of nowhere, a cold wind comes up suddenly, whips across the trees by the roadside and pounds on my window. I feel the biting chill and I tell myself, winter is coming. I recall the weather forecast the day before, predicting colder days.

The vicious wind shakes the trees wildly. Tree leaves, still green, fall off, swirl and shower down on top of the cars waiting for the light change at the intersection. Some of the leaves hang on for dear life and refuse to part from the limb—like toddlers refusing to let go of their mother's hand. I think of my children when they were little.

I look at all the fallen leaves and feel sorry for the street sweepers who must come out in the freezing cold at dawn. The sudden change of weather has caught people unprepared, not only the sweepers but the men who had gone to work dressed in light clothes this morning. I imagine briefly that the women and children of those men will meet them with a heavy coat at the subway station around quitting time, a beautiful sight to behold.

Most people like autumn. Ancient poets have praised autumn, the season of tall sky and food aplenty. I think the poets preferred autumn to the spring season. You don't have to be a poet to become inspired by autumn, when its pristine air displaces the heat of summer. Farmers celebrate harvest and write poetry of their own.

But I never liked autumn... not the season itself, but the tears mother had shed come autumn. When the leaves fell and rolled around in the courtyard, my mother would sit on the veranda and weep, forgetting how cold it was. I couldn't stand her when she did this. I'd to stay late in school. Looking back, I think I was an odd child, staying away from mother when she needed me the most.

It took me a lifetime to realize what mother was going through. Like the sole leaf hanging onto the persimmon tree in the wind, she was trying to hang on to her last bits of memory of my father. She was expressing herself through her tears, the only means available to her.

As for me, I try my hand at writing. I try to express myself in words rather than tears. I start writing what's in my heart, the truth. But sometimes, I am tempted to compromise myself, especially when the truth would put me in disadvantage. I bend the truth or skirt around it and frankly, my essays read more genuine than what I feel. I hate myself when this happens and I feel like hanging up my pen these days.

But I hang on. Like the last persimmon leaf. If the last leaf falls and tumbles down to the ground, I think I'd cry, too.

Outing

My brother and I decided to take our mother to Chonan Memorial Park. I prepared some snacks and fruits as if we were going on a picnic. We weren't going on a real picnic—we were on our way to visit the cemetery in Chonan, where we had bought a plot for mother's final resting place.

The idea of buying a cemetery plot for mother came from my aunt. She and mother were talking one day, when mother lamented that she had no place to rest after her death. My aunt called me and hinted that we should prepare a plot for mother.

So my brother paid for the 216 square-foot site and I paid for a dress she would wear to her grave. I didn't feel comfortable getting ready for her passing, even though it was inevitable. These were our meager gifts for her after what she had done for us all her life.

Mother, on the other hand, was comfortable with the idea and she was anxious to see her plot. She surprised me. She has never been one to worry about her future. She has always focused on the present.

As her children, we try our best to make her life comfortable, but she doesn't always agree with us. She lives alone now, about an hour away from me. My husband and I tried to talk to her about living with us, but she refused. My brother had talked her into living with him in America. But she didn't last one year there. She said, "I don't understand a word, I don't speak a word there. I have no ears, no mouth. Life is not worth living there. I'd rather find my way in my own land, eat whatever I want to, whenever I want to, instead of depending on someone else for everything."

Obviously, she wants to be her own person, but I have difficulty in accepting her wish. After she moved back from America, my brother and his wife have taken turns visiting mother and staying with her months at a time. Mother's friends envy her, but she is not happy that they spend so much money flying back and forth from America just for her. My brother is flying back to America in a few days, and we are going to check on mother's plot together before he goes, the three of us together like the old days. This outing may be the last time we are together.

Two hours later, we enter the Memorial Park. The park feels quiet and peaceful. Cows graze in the meadow in the distance, and reeds sway in autumn breeze. Critters chirp in the grass field nearby as we reach her plot. The area is manicured meticulously. To her right side, stands a new, shiny tombstone. Mother has a new neighbor. Mother smiles and sighs, "My resting place..." as she pounds her feet all around the plot.

We spread out a blanket and sit down for a picnic. Mother smiles, enjoying her food. My brother and I watch her quietly.

Cicada

Early morning cicada in the hill in front chirps, rings throughout the house. It's the cicada season aftermath of a monsoon. One starts singing here and another follows there and another, and soon, it's a full-blown chorus. They persist, and at times, their insistence annoys me, when suddenly they stop as if on cue. They aren't so unpleasant, after all, I think. That's how it is with cicadas. Autumn night crickets fill you with melancholy while cicadas in the heat of summer sing of youth, revitalize the senses laying dormant inside.

According to biologists, male cicadas cry to attract females and to mobilize comrades of like species. Cicada species come in two types: maemi and sseureurami. Maemi belts out a sound that begins with m, followed by a vowel ae then closed by m, thus the name maemi. Sseureurami cries ssrr ssrr ssrr. Whoever named these critters, I think they are very appropriate.

The sound of these critters in the heat of summer has a cooling effect on me, like the arias Maria Callas sings. With the pollution problem worsening each day, I feel fortunate that these insects continue to survive and sing for us. Once I drove my car on a hot day to attend some urgent business. The street was jammed like a parking lot, filled with hot exhaust fumes. The stop-and-go traffic was nothing but aggravation for me and everyone else stuck in it. Just then a maemi in a tree by the roadway sang, as refreshing as the sound of a rain shower in the middle of a forest or ocean waves breaking by the shore. The maemi sound melted away my tenseness from sitting in the horrific traffic jam and the rude drivers who nosed their way into my lane.

Listening to the maemi sing, I was reminded of the story my grandmother told me when I was young. A long time ago, there was a bookworm of a scholar who devoted himself to his studies and nothing else. Come rain or shine, he had his nose buried in his books and he didn't know or care if his grains were washed away in a storm. Owing to his devotion, he managed to pass his civil service examination, the only means available for commoners to attain a position in the society in those days. He did achieve his goal, but his wife had passed away in the meantime. It is said that her spirit turned into maemi's songs, and together with croaking frogs, they sing songs and pray for rain.

The ancient Confucian scholars attached various meanings to maemi: they called it mun (文) to depict its shape resembling the tie strings hanging from the headgear of a literati; cheong (淸) to signify its purity from consuming only dewdrops; yeom (廉) to signify the fact that it doesn't harm grains and other farm products. Further, maemi represents geom (儉) for its frugal way of living without building an elaborate habitat, and shin (信) for exercising moderation, seasonal shedding of its shell. All together, these five virtues in maemi were deemed as exemplary virtues for gentlemen scholars to follow.

I read an ancient poem about maemi and reflect on maemi's life cycle on this earth.

> I heard maemi sing
> clear voice so enticing
> I wanted it for my own.
> Maemi was oblivious,
> sensed no danger;
> only the pleasure of
> celebrating brevity of existence.
> Maemi,
> I see you now and
> I know what I must do:
> I shall guard myself against my own vanity.

When I was a child, I used to tie a string to a maemi and let it fly around like a kite. Little did I know that the maemi spent seventeen years in a cocoon under the earth before it surfaced above ground for two more cycles of transformation—just to sing for one summer season. Buddhists regarded the maemi's life cycle as a symbol of reincarnation, and killing maemi was taboo. Ever since I learned about maemi's significance, I have felt bad about my cruel treatment of maemi as a child.

My sense of guilt stays with me, and I feel nonplussed when I see disparaging references to maemi, such as wa myung seon ryun (蛙鳴蟬聯), meaning the crying noises of frogs and maemi. The phrase refers to a person who writes in a disorganized manner, filled with useless theories. It also associates maemi with noisy gibberish, and I resent the implication.

A biologist told me once that male maemi must sing louder than ever before in order to make him heard over the noise pollution nowadays. They know that nature is deteriorating and they are adapting themselves to the new ways.

The maemi in the persimmon tree by the kitchen stops singing, trailing off weakly. It sounds like a complaint, maybe a scream — that if it doesn't survive this harsh world, humans can't make it, either.

Women of Three Generations

I had long ignored my doctor's advice to lessen my load in life and continued to extend myself until I discovered for myself one day that my body was not as strong as it used to be. My doctor had known all along that registering blood pressure past 180 meant a red light, a warning signal. I finally relented and passed on my duties of carrying out the family rituals honoring ancestors, *jesa*, after forty years. I relegated to my oldest child the *jesa* duties for the new years and for my mother-in-law. To my second child, I assigned the *jesa* duties for chuseok rituals earmarked for the harvest season in the fall and for my father-in-law. Thus, tremendous weight was lifted off my shoulders.

So I thought.

Instead of a sense of liberation, I feel lost, inexplicably. Sometimes, I regret that I had abandoned my duty as the woman of the family.

Looking back to my early years of marriage, I must admit that I had been overwhelmed by the weight of the *jesa* rituals. I had married into a family that observed *jesa* religiously, thus inheriting the responsibilities.

I hadn't grown up with the *jesa* tradition in my own family; my mother was under the opinion that *jesa* rituals for the dead were useless. She used to say, "Don't perform any *jesa* for me after I die. Presenting a bowl of water to parents while they are alive means much more than an elaborate ritual after they're dead."

Her words had left an impression on me, and I had vowed not to marry into a family that performed *jesa*. Well, that didn't work.

My husband had come home early one day and informed me of the *jesa* we were to perform. He proceeded to tell me what dishes to offer on the *jesa* table, steamed rice and soup, which I was to refer to as "mae" and "gang" respectively. And he went on to instruct me on the rest of the menu. "You have to offer a plate of jujube fruit. Jujube has a single seed, which symbolizes the royalty line. I know it's hard to find a nice pear, but do your best. The pear's yellow skin means brightness, and its white meat stands for purity. Together, they represent our Korean character. Don't forget to put out persimmon. Persimmon reminds us about pain. We become whole only after we learn to withstand the pains of life. You must put out okdom, Jeju's unique fish. Never put out any fish without scales."

I replied, "I'll do as you say," incredibly. I should have been angry. I should have felt cheated that the burden had fallen on me, especially when I had married him because he was a third son. The tradition called for the first son to perform *jesa* duties.

Nonetheless, I took on the additional task as a dutiful wife—at one word from my husband—with religious devotion. I would mark the *jesa* dates on the calendar with a red pen and start my count-down one month in advance. I soaked dried fern stems in water, changing water everyday so they wouldn't spoil. Without a refrigerator in those days, I had to be careful in planning the *jesa* menu, what I could make ahead of time and could not. With one day left to go, I would start boiling meats and frying tofu and fish cubes, filling the house with cooking smell. I stacked bits of fried foods in bamboo baskets and stored them in cool spots away from the sun, as well as my children who craved snacks all the time.

I slapped their hands and chased them away, telling them that the food was an offering to their grandfather's spirit and not mere snacks. They should treat the food with reverence, I told them. My friend and helper said that grandfather's spirit wouldn't mind if his grandchildren sampled the *jesa* food ahead of time. In fact, he would be very pleased, she said.

My granddaughter and I go for a walk in the park now and then, where I see newlyweds take pictures. I see elated brides dressed in white gowns and wonder if they would abide by their husbands' words like I had. Things have changed drastically now, and I hear that some people conduct *jesa* at fancy hotels with catered menus these days. They merely substitute the names of the ancestors to be memorialized, Kim or Lee, whatever, without any regard for the family traditions that were handed down the line. I am appalled to hear about the "formula" *jesa* and I hope it is not true.

Today, my first son is conducting *jesa* for my mother-in-law. Many candles burn over the *jesa* table, and incense smell fills the room. Calligraphy (brush-work on rice paper by my father-in-law) hangs on the folding screen in front, depicting the departed soul of my mother-in-law. I sit on the floor with my legs folded under me. My son pours rice wine into a cup.

My father-in-law takes the wine cup, raises it over the incense bowl, swings the cup in a slow circular motion around the incense bowl, and places the cup on the altar. He steps back, kneels to the floor, places his hands on the floor, and bows, his forehead almost touching the back of his hands. He stands up and bows once more and stays still in a bow. My two sons stand crouched in a low bow one step behind my father-in-law. Suddenly, my three-year-old grandson goes up behind his grandfather and mimics a bow. Women in the kitchen try not to laugh. I'm thinking that my mother-in-law's spirit is smiling.

The Wealthy

The Ryu family of Gu-Re in Jeon Nam Province is said to have shared their crop with their neighbors. The Ryu family took what they needed for the winter and put the remainder outside with a sign for strangers to take what they needed. The Ryu's left the crop unattended so that the takers could remain anonymous.

This sort of magnanimity is rare in the dog-eat-dog world we live in these days. We live in a world of struggles — between farmers and the government, labor versus management, and the have's against the have-not's.

The so-called labor movement we see today go against all the moral principles and wisdom that we have inherited from our ancestors. Often, the labor organizations strike and wear red bands around their heads and shout hostile slogans. It is war, and I wonder if our nation can survive such bitterness. What happened to the cooperative spirit from the days when we had fought to recover our nation from the Japanese invasion?

I visited Tiaowi Fortress in the Tsechuan District of China last summer. I stood at the gate where the Mongols had made two hundred take-over attempts over a thirty-six year period in the 13th century. All the traces of the brutal battles have given way to green moss on its walls now. It was also a site where Chiang Kai Shek used to train military officers against the Japanese invaders in the 1930s, according to a sign that I saw.

The sign also said that Koreans had trained there as well, and I felt certain sadness for our bygone patriots who had shed blood and sweat to recover our lost country. Their spirits were still present. I felt worried and concerned for the well being of our fatherland.

Sadly, I don't see the same concern for our fatherland today and I feel ashamed in the eyes of our forefathers who had fought to regain our tiny nation. Solidarity and a united spirit are things of the past, and our society is engaged in a battle of selfish greed. Despite the economic miracle and new wealth, we have our share of poverty in our society. Instead of addressing the poverty issues and finding solutions for the poor, the so-called leaders are conducting a dangerous political game in the name of populism. They have openly pitted the have's against the have-not's by labeling the achievers as the main cause for the woes of the underachievers.

Their basic approach to "the solution" has been to "take from the rich and give to the poor," which might have sounded attractive during the elections, but in reality, these gouging-the-rich policies have produced maleficent results. Instead of narrowing the disparity of wealth, the poor have become poorer. At this rate, I am afraid that the entire nation will turn poorer for the sake of the equal distribution of wealth.

I am thinking of a story of a rich family named Choi, who had maintained their family wealth spanning over twelve generations (from 1600 to 1900). They did this by sharing the crop with the less fortunate and adhering to moral principles. The Choi family philosophy mandated clear separation of economics and politics for the men. Men were encouraged to serve the king by passing the qualification examination for public service. They were not to seek the top government posts, however. Also, the family never bought land during drought years, when farmers were forced to sell their farmland well below its true value. Every year, they would set aside 1,000 seok of rice (about 50 tons; 1 seok is a straw sack equivalent to 2.1 cubic feet) to feed wayfarers that would visit the house during the coming year. They routinely shared any profit over 10,000 seok from a given rice farm, and villagers everywhere welcomed the Choi family.

I am forever moved by the wisdom of our ancestors and I long to see the same wisdom in the world today.

Mother's House

The funeral parlor rang with Christian hymns; no incense burned. Over fifty people were there, holding a memorial service in front of mother's effigy. I had flown to America the moment I had received the telephone call about her failing condition, but I arrived too late. She had gone to the other side by the time I got here.The memorial service was finished according to the schedule (arranged by the funeral director according the American custom) and everyone went off on their own way. This custom was new to me, as I expected the mourners to keep mother's spirit company, the Korean custom. If there were purgatory, her spirit would be lingering on about this time.

Everyone left, and we came home to my brother's house, empty and sad without mother and a crowd of mourners. Come morning, they'll bury her body in the ground, and she will be on her lonely road never to return, I was thinking. People consoled me, pointed out that she had a full life of eighty-nine years. But there was no way they could know what a lonely life she had led against all odds. She had never gotten her one remaining wish in life— return to her home in Korea after her recovery— and I couldn't stop crying for her.

After her first stroke, she had managed to ask me, slurring her words, "Do people die in America, too?" This was not a simple question; I knew what she was thinking. She wanted to believe that she was going recover her health and return to her home in Korea after her treatment in America. She meant to come home afterwards, and I knew this was foremost in her mind as she went to America with my brother.

She wouldn't be able to stay away from her small traditional home with the old style smoke chimney, probably the last remaining in metropolitan Seoul then. That was where she had sustained her dreams and stored her memories. She always stoked a fire in her old fire pit in the kitchen, be it for boiling bath water or making a bowl of rice. Perhaps her stubborn streak might have been at work trying to assuage her loneliness while she raised two children as a widow. I'd suggest a new kitchen for her, but she always refused. That was where she'd made soup for her grandchildren, made rice, and steamed vegetables.

Step inside the gate at her house, you saw a chord of firewood, her treasure. She made certain that she had plenty of wood, and her stackof firewood had a way of growing taller. When I stopped in at her house once in a while, she would emerge out of her kitchen as she wiped her wet hands, beaming like a new bride, never showing any sign of loneliness in her face. I remember thinking that I should live carefree just like her.

I remember visiting her in America for the first time. She had been waiting by the window for my arrival and when we drove up, she came out to the front yard, hugged me, and cried, so happy to see me. Her tears also spoke of her lonely life in the strange land as well, I felt.

I looked around to see a beautiful home surrounded by a park-like setting, the immaculate grass lawn, roses, gladiolas, cherry blossoms, and the tree lined streets.

I told her, "Mom, it's so nice here. I should pack up everything and come here and live near you." She pursed her lips and stuttered, "What's so good about it? My own shack back home is the best."

The second visit was at the end of August. The trees lining the streets from the airport to home glittered healthy in the sun, and I thought that the healthy environment in America would bring back mother's health for sure. I stepped inside the house and called out "Mom" like a child, but mother in her bed barely managed to hold up her arm and give me a weak smile.

I lay down next to her holding her hand, and she'd mutter unintelligibly late into the night. She was telling me a long story, yet I couldn't understand a word she was saying.

On my third visit, mother didn't recognize me. She'd given me a smile, but it was a smile directed at an acquaintance, not her daughter.

I yelled, "I'm your loving daughter" as I hugged her. She ignored me and said, "There, there, a man in dark clothes."

Then I mimicked a shaman and danced around the room, hollering, "Disappear! Go away!" at the invisible shadow that pestered mother. After a while, she'd let out a long sigh of relief. I knew then that she didn't have too much time left. At times when she'd regained her wits, she was surprised to see me and said, "What are you doing here? Let's go home to Seoul."

The morning after the funeral service, the drizzle stopped. A cloud floated by in the blue sky this late autumn day. People sang the hymn of farewell and the pallbearers loaded mother's casket in the hearse.

In my brother's car behind the hearse I closed my eyes. Mother's image looms: she is dressed nice in her traditional garb, her beaming face filled with excitement. She's going home, she says. She doesn't know: her old house has been torn down, replaced by a high-rise. I am overcome with new sadness for her lonesome journey. A gloomy shadow falls over mother's apparition.